AF251912

CHARACTERISTICS
Of The Present Political State
Of Great Britain

Also Published in

REPRINTS OF ECONOMIC CLASSICS

By ROBERT WALLACE

A Dissertation on the Numbers of Mankind [1809]

Various Prospects of Mankind, Nature and
Providence [1761]

[ROBERT WALLACE]

CHARACTERISTICS

OF THE

PRESENT POLITICAL STATE

OF

GREAT BRITAIN

[1758]

REPRINTS OF ECONOMIC CLASSICS

AUGUSTUS M. KELLEY · PUBLISHERS
NEW YORK 1969

First Edition 1761

(London: *Printed for* A. Millar *in the Strand,* 1761)

Reprinted 1969 by

AUGUSTUS M. KELLEY · PUBLISHERS
NEW YORK NEW YORK 10010

LIBRARY OF CONGRESS CATALOGUE CARD NUMBER

69-19551

PRINTED IN THE UNITED STATES OF AMERICA
by SENTRY PRESS, NEW YORK, N. Y. 10019

CHARACTERISTICS

OF THE

Prefent Political State

OF

GREAT BRITAIN.

Prifca juvent alios: ego me nunc denique natum
Gratulor. OVID.

The SECOND EDITION,
With Corrections and Additions by the Author.

LONDON:

Printed for A. MILLAR in the Strand.
MDCCLVIII.

THE
CONTENTS.

CONTENTS.

E R R A T A.

Page 33. laft line for *of France* read *in France*.
74. In the note, line 7. for *an* read *on*.
81. line 18. for *no* read *not*.
84. line 6. for *bad* read *a bad*.
Ibid line 24. for *fituation* read *fituations*.
89. line 7. for *free* read *a free*.
96. line 22. for *ommerce* read *commerce*.
114. line 9. for *his* read *this*.
118. line 12. for *fo poor* read *poor*.
124. firft line in the note, for *the* read *in the*.
164. line 1. for *the* read *their*.
167. line 7. for *the fwooning* read *and of fwooning*.
174. In the note, line 7. for *the* read *that the*.
Ibid. in the note, laft line, for *this* read *his*.
176. line 20. for *uniform* read *univerfal*.
187. line 15. for *the* read *their*.

A D V E R-

ADVERTISEMENT.

THE following Characteristics were written in order to give a more just and a more agreeable prospect of the present state of Britain, than is to be seen in many late writings. The author hopes, they will contribute something to remove the disquiet of good citizens, and to defeat the designs of the disaffected.

HAVING conceived a very favourable opinion of the revolution in the year 1688, and of the British government ever since that period; having been confirmed in this opinion by observing the happiness of the people, and by comparing the condition of Britain with that of other nations; he has often been surprised at those loud complaints, which are made of our poverty, of our want of silver and gold, of the abuse of paper credit, the greatness of our taxes, the loss of our trade, and the great increase of the national debts: all said to be occasioned by a series of mismanagements ever since the Revolution. Complaints of this kind tend naturally to disquiet the friends of

the

the conftitution, and furnifh its fecret enemies with many topics of declamation to
create and to fupport difaffection.

But, what is ftill more aftonifhing and
alarming, it has been of late publickly
afferted, that our national genius and capacity are almoft quite gone ; and that we
are grown fo feeble both in our counfels,
and in the execution of them, that we run
the greateft rifk of becoming an eafy prey
to any bold invader.

This debility is *faid* to flow immediately
from our luxury, and from the effeminacy
of our manners ; but is fuppofed to be originally derived from the reftraints laid on
the royal prerogative, from the new dignity
and power acquired by our parliaments, and
from the acceffion of liberty gained by the
people at the Revolution. In confequence
of this alteration in our political fyftem, our
princes having too little power, and the people too much liberty ; liberty has degenerated into licentioufnefs ; and there is nothing
now to be found in our conftitution, able
to give a fufficient check to the natural bad
confequences of luxury and of effeminacy.
Hence, as is afferted, we are upon the
brink of a precipice, and going faft to def-
ftruction.

Tho

THO thofe gentlemen, who, on the one fide, complain fo loudly of our poverty, and thofe, who, on the other, make as loud complaints of the bad effects of our riches, are very oppofite in their principles; they agree, however, in the fame conclufion. The one party affirm, that we are ruined by poverty; the other impute our ruin to our riches; but both maintain, that we *are* ruined, and, in fome fort, connect this ruin with the Revolution.

EXCITED by a natural curiofity to find out the truth in a matter of fuch importance; anxious for the welfare of his country; the author of thefe Characteriftics fet himfelf to enquire, whether there was juft ground for fuch complaints; or whether the nation is not at prefent much richer, happier, and more powerful, than it was before the Revolution. Having examined impartially what might be faid on both fides, he hath compofed the little treatife that follows, and prefumes to offer it to the Public at a crifis fo important and fo interefting.

BEING neither merchant, manufacturer, nor farmer; having no management of the revenue, nor any fhare in public counfels; he thinks himfelf obliged to own, that he

has

has no other means of being inftructed in the ftate of the nation, than fuch as are open to every other gentleman. He therefore brings his arguments chiefly from what is *obvious* and *vifible*. It might indeed be an advantage, if either gentlemen who are converfant in commerce and manufactures, or fuch as are concerned in the revenue, would publifh fome of their anecdotes that are not among the *arcana imperii*. By a comparifon of the prefent ftate of their country, with its ftate before the Revolution, they could eafily refute thofe falfe allegations concerning its poverty. However, it may be poffible to do without them. The poverty and the riches of a nation muft be, in fome fort, *fenfible*. At leaft, they may be difcerned by a *careful* obferver. Nay, one may argue concerning them, perhaps, with greater certainty, from obvious appearances, than from the moft minute accounts of taxes and of the public revenue. Of the condition of a nation in *other* refpects, we muft be able to form the fureft judgment from what is obvious and vifible.

ONE who reafons in this manner, concerning the riches or the happinefs of a country, *from what is fenfible*; acts much like an audience, who judge of the merit of a play, or of an oration, by their inward

ward

ward feelings.   If they find themselves greatly interested, they conclude that the poet or the orator is a master.   But it will be difficult to convince them, from the rules of criticism, that a piece is excellent, if even when they are in a temper the moft fuited to feel the force of it, they find themfelves cold and languid, notwithftanding all the efforts of the author.   In like manner, it may be concluded, that when a nation is encreafing in riches, and is living at eafe, the effects of its profperity muft be vifible and fenfible.

But there is fcarce any audience, in which one will not meet either with fome four ill-natured people, who are *fond* of finding fault; or with fome, who are fo full of *vanity* and *affectation*, that they like to contradict the *common* opinion; or with fome, who through melancholy, or other diforders of body or mind, are not in a proper difpofition to be duly affected. Something of the fame kind often happens in the State.   Tho the great body of the people are fenfible of their own happinefs, many fhall be found of fuch four and fuch peevifh difpofitions, or fo blinded with prejudices, or fo fretted by difappointments, or of fuch timorous and anxious tempers, that they will be continually *imagining* within them-

felves,

felves, and, if they live under a free government, and in a learned age, will endeavour by their converfation and by their
writings to perfuade others, that all things
are in the greateft diforder, and that the
happieft nation in the world is haftening to
perdition.

THE good-natured part of mankind,
no doubt, will agree in pitying fuch unfortunate and anxious citizens, for fancying
to themfelves fo many *imaginary* evils, and
for undertaking the difficult tafk of per-
fuading others out of their fenfes, or of
making a nation believe that it is extremely poor and oppreffed, when, in truth, it
is rich and free. But there is not the fame
agreement among politicians about the manner, in which fuch peevifh writings ought
to be treated. Some think it beft to defpife
them altogether, both becaufe they aim
at an impoffibility, to wit, to convince a
powerful and a happy people, that they are
weak and miferable; and becaufe there is
feldom any reafon to hope that either the
authors themfelves, or fuch as have adopt-
ed their opinions, will ever be convinced of
their errors. This is faid to be the cafe
with all controverfial writers and their writings; the former are never to be convinced; the latter have no effect on either fide.
The

The opinions and the principles of men are formed by other means.

BUT ftrong objections lie againft the policy of this *principle*. Eooks, pamphlets, fongs, are known, from experience, to have confiderable influence both in forming and in confirming the opinions of mankind. They have produced fignal effects in the world. It muft therefore be dangerous in any Government, it muft be fo efpecially in a free one, to neglect altogether the compofitions which are publifhed without regard to the ftrain in which they are written. Like company, if they are of a peevifh gloomy complexion, they are infectious, and tend to four the minds of the people. Befides, the falfe opinions of men may be corrected, if objects are fhewn them in a proper light. The world is far from being fo bad as many imagine. Many have a fincere defire to find out the truth. Tho they have been blinded by prejudices, they are capable of conviction. For their fake the truth ought to be fairly expofed to public view.

IT is for thefe reafons, that the author of the Characteriftics has propofed to give a more comfortable, and, as he thinks, a

more

more juſt view of the ſtate of the Public, than is to be ſeen in ſeveral late writings.

THE writings, on which this author is to offer ſome animadverſions, relate to our paper-credit, to our taxes, to the public debts, to our luxury, to our effeminacy, and to a variety of other political ſubjects. They have been compoſed with very different intentions. Some of them by friends of the Government, without any bad deſign; others, as it is viſible, by its ſecret enemies, with an intention, not only to foment faction, but to promote diſaffection. If we ſhall believe ſome of theſe writers, the nation has, ever ſince the Revolution, been in a poor and wretched ſtate. It is ſo at preſent, and all things are going to ruin. Inſtead of ſilver and gold, we have nothing but paper-credit. Our *banks* are pernicious, and are ſigns of our poverty. Our *taxes* are heavier than we can bear. They render it impoſſible for us to carry on trade to advantage; they have made us loſe much of it already, and as they raiſe the prices of proviſions and labour, they muſt make us gradually loſe the remainder of it, and be under-ſold by other nations in all the markets of the world. Our *public debts* too are certain proofs of our low condition; ſince we are obliged to borrow, and cannot

raiſe

raife the fums neceffary for the public fervice, within the year. They could never
have rifen fo high, unlefs we had been moft
miferably oppreffed by the Government,
and are fo great, that we fhall never be able
to pay them : indeed, they ought not to be
paid, but to be abolifhed at once by act of
parliament; with a few merciful exceptions,
in favour of widows, of orphans, and of
fuch others as deferve compaffion. Nay,
according to fome of thefe gentlemen, our
agriculture is making very flow advances.
Notwithftanding all which difadvantages,
they affert, at the fame time, that we are
fwimming in all kinds of foreign luxury.
Thus one fort of writers.

There are others, who go upon a different fyftem. They confefs that we are both
rich and free. They even allow that we are
poffeffed of an extenfive trade, have acquired immenfe wealth, and enjoy the moft
ample liberty. But they maintain, at the
fame time, that our liberty has degenerated
into licentioufnefs ; that it has produced an
effeminacy of manners, extinguifhed the
good principles, and deftroyed the genius
and capacity, of the nation, to fuch a degree, that we are now become defencelefs,
and run the greateft hazard of falling before the fuperior genius of the French.

IN oppofition to both thefe kinds of writers, who exhibit fuch a difagreeable picture
of the prefent age, the writer of the Characteriftics endeavours to fhew, That Britain
is in an opulent condition at prefent, and
has been very happy ever fince the Revolution : That banking is a very profitable inftitution, and has greatly enriched the nation : That, tho our taxes are high, we
are much richer, than we were when they
were much lower ; and carry on an extenfive and profitable trade : That, tho the
greatnefs of the public debt muft be a confiderable lofs, we both are rich and free at
prefent, and may continue hereafter to be
rich, and to enjoy the moft perfect liberty
and fecurity of any nation in the world :
That the propofal to abolifh the public
debts, without paying them, is neither juft
nor profitable : That every farthing of them
ought to be paid, and may be paid without
any diftrefs to the nation ; and that, notwithftanding the juft complaints of our
luxury, effeminacy, and corruption, we
have fufficient means of felf-defence, and
are fully able to fupport ourfelves againft
the French, or any nation whatever. Thefe
are the chief topics infifted on in the Characteriftics. The author has digefted his
reflections into the order, which he thinks
moft proper for fetting the prefent ftate of
the

the nation in a juft light.   He doth not in-
tend his work as an anfwer to any piece
whatfoever; yet he takes the liberty to ani-
madvert on the writings of other Gentlemen, as they chance to ftand in his way, or
have afferted contrary principles.   Nor hath
he fcrupled, from fear of the imputation
of pedantry, to refer to the paffages of
their books at the bottom of the page.

It is mean to flatter any court, any faction, or any perfon whatever.   Therefore,
how greatly foever he efteems the government or the times fince the Revolution, he
will be far from maintaining, either that
the adminiftration has been guilty of *no*
errors fince that remarkable æra; or that
there is not an odd concurrence of perplex-
ing circumftances in our prefent condition.
Neverthelefs, from a fincere love to his
country, he thinks himfelf obliged to maintain, that, notwithftanding all errors, which
either are committed by the Government at
prefent, or have been committed by it during the laft feventy years, Britain is much
richer, is much more fecure, and enjoys
many more advantages, than in any former
period : And that, notwithftanding fome
unlucky events and difappointments in the
courfe of the prefent war, the nation is
fully

fully able to defend itſelf againſt all its enemies.

NEITHER will any wiſe man, out of his
zeal for the Revolution, which was founded on liberty, adopt the ſlaviſh doctrine,
that a true patriot ſhould not *take notice* of
ſuch errors as have been committed ſince
that happy æra. On the contrary, the
wiſeſt and beſt friends of the Revolution
will ever be the moſt ſincere lovers of liberty. Therefore, they will be the moſt ſtre-
nuous ſupporters of the liberty of the preſs,
and will boldly maintain, againſt all flatterers and time-pleaſers, that the people of
Great Britain *have a right* to take notice of
errors in the adminiſtration, to point them
out to public view, and to lay them before
their repreſentatives in parliament.

BUT liberty may degenerate into licenti-
ouſneſs. Some diſcontented writers have
gone too far. One ought not wantonly to
ſuggeſt, that the public credit is in danger,
or, like the writer of three late Eſſays *, to
make a propoſal for erecting ſocieties, which

---

* The firſt on the public debt; the ſecond on paper-money, banking, &c; and the third on frugality; ſaid in the title page to have been printed at
London, 1755.

ſhall

fhall circulate no bank-notes, but at an advanced price. Such a propofal feems to to be too affuming. It tends to create imaginary fears, gives falfe alarms, and can be excufed only on the fuppofition, that it will be without effect. With how much greater prudence, as well as pious affection to his country, does the public-fpirited author of the Querift * put the following query, " Whether the credit of the public funds " be not a mine of gold to England; and " whether any ftep, that fhould leffen this " credit, ought not to be dreaded?" How different is this gentleman from the writer of the Three Effays, who, with an unufual vehemence, calls upon the landed gentlemen, upon the farmers, and upon the manufacturers, to put an end to our paper-credit altogether.

It is ftill more dangerous and inexcufable, like the author of a late Eftimate, to aggravate our vices and our weakneffes fo much beyond the truth, as naturally tends to difpirit our countrymen, and to raife the fpirits of the French. During many years, the writer of the Characteriftics has been forry to *read* fuch melancholy and unfavou-

* The no lefs ingenious than pious Bifhop of Cloyne. See the 233d Query of the Querift, 5th edition, printed 1750.

rable

rable accounts of the ſtate of the Public. But, after the daſtardiſing repreſentations given by the author of the Eſtimate, he could no longer forbear to *publiſh* his thoughts, and to draw his pen in the ſervice of his country.

PART

PART I.

Of Banks, and of Paper-Credit.

IN order to form a true judgment of the political ſtate of Great Britain, it is neceſſary to conſider the nature of Paper-credit, and to enquire whether Banks are uſeful or dangerous to a nation.

One would think, the advantages of Banks muſt have been ſo manifeſt from *experience*, that, long before this time, no doubt could have been entertained of their uſefulneſs. But, inſtead of any univerſal agreement in their favour, ſuch violent prejudices have been contracted againſt them, that not the vulgar alone who have never conſidered the ſubject, but ſome very inquiſitive and ingenious gentlemen, have fallen into conſiderable miſtakes in this matter, and look on Banks as detrimental to trade and induſtry.

However, as *experience* hath convinced the *trading part* of the world of the advantages of Banking; it will not be difficult to ſhew, *from the nature of the thing,* in

what

what manner Banks become ufeful in commerce.

IN a nation that is chiefly addicted to a-
griculture and to pafturage, where the people, fatisfying themfelves with a fimple
life, and wanting only a few conveniencies,
deal but little in trade and in manufactures;
money will not be very neceffary.   Much
of their commerce may be carried on by
barter.   But, where there is a great variety of manufactures and commodities,
where all forts of arts are encouraged, and
where elegance is ftudied; much money
will not only be *profitable*, but be *abfolutely neceffary* for the exigencies of the ftate.

HOWEVER, there *may be* too much money in a nation.   And there is certainly too
much, if it renders the great body of the
people idle, and enables them to purchafe
what they want, from foreigners, without
any labour or induftry of their own.   This
was the cafe with Spain, two or three hundred years ago, and did great harm to that
country.   But it will fcarce be poffible to
procure fo much money by trade alone.

INDUSTRY and labour are far better than
money, and will foon be able to procure it
in exchange for commodities.   Yet induftry
ftands

ftands fometimes in need to be *quickened*; and money is very ferviceable for this purpofe.

LET us fuppofe, that there is a certain quantity of money and of commodities in any country. The quantity of money may be faid to reprefent the commodities, and to determine the prices of them. The prices of *particular* commodities may vary in different circumftances; but, if the *fums* of the money and of the commodities continue much *the fame*, the prices, *on the whole*, cannot much alter. In fuch a cafe, if no more money comes into the country, unlefs the difpofitions of the people are remarkably changed by fome extraordinary accident or revolution, it will be very difficult to carry on a great deal of more work on a fudden, or fpeedily to increafe the fum of the commodities.

BUT, if a great fum of money fhould be brought into the nation at once, and be diftributed any way whatever, provided the labouring and induftrious part of the nation do not get fuch fums as will keep them idle; though fome part of it would undoubtedly be hoarded up, and would thereby be rendered ufelefs, yet the greateft part of it would be employed, and become ufeful. The great people would immediately

lay

lay out part of it in adding to their houfes, to their furniture, to their equipages, and to their tables. The merchants and manufacturers would employ more hands, and carry on a greater trade. The farmers would improve their lands. The graziers would breed a greater and a better ftock of cattle. Every one would be enabled to fpend a little more, and to carry on his bufinefs better. By thefe means there would be every where more labour. Of courfe, the commodities, or *real* riches, which are quite *different* from *money*, would be greatly increafed.

AGAIN : If the ftock of money fhould be increafed by this induftry : or, if *another fum* of money fhould be introduced by other means, and be diftributed as before; this would again increafe the ftock of commodities. And fo on continually, or to a certain limit.

Now, Banks, fettled by public authority under right regulations, continually increafe the current fpecies, by iffuing notes which circulate as money. By giving credit, they furnifh men of fubftance with the means of giving greater employment to the induftrious, and enable merchants to carry on a more extenfive trade. The more notes

the

the Banks can circulate in this way, the more will induſtry and trade be promoted. Nor can there be any limit, while the borrowers from theſe banks can give good ſecurity, and the managers take care to iſſue no more notes, than, by experience they have learned, they can anſwer, according to the ordinary courſe of demand. Whatever ſums landed men, merchants, or others, borrow, provided they can give good ſecurity, and borrow on reaſonable proſpects; this is ſo far from being a loſs, that it increaſes induſtry and conſumption. A great quantity of Bank-notes only ſhews, that great ſums have been borrowed by one part of the nation from another, upon good ſecurity, for carrying on trade, and for other reaſonable purpoſes : Which is ſo far from being either a ſign, or the cauſe, of poverty, that it is both the ſign, and a mean, of greater riches.

It is of no conſequence, in this argument, that there may be more paper-money than ſilver and gold, and that the proportion betwixt them may not be aſcertained ; provided the former regulations are duly obſerved.

It is of no conſequence that foreign nations will not take our *Bank-notes*. They
will

will take our *goods*, which are produced by the circulation of thefe notes among our-felves.

IT is of no confequence, though the value of the Bank-notes fhould happen to extend to a vaft fum, provided the Banks, which are to anfwer thefe notes, have an equal value in coin, bullion, lands, goods, and good debts, to which there is convenient accefs.

IT is of no confequence, though landed men mortgage part of their eftates for Bank-notes, and may be faid to coin their lands, and to bring them into the market. On the contrary, the more the lands of any country are *locked up*, the country muft be lefs improved. And the more eafily lands can be transferred and exchanged in commerce; induftry, trade, and manufactures will be more fpeedily and fuccefsfully promoted.

BANKS are not only *profitable*, but may be faid, in many cafes, to be *neceffary*. When a fpirit of induftry is any way excited in a nation, if, by this induftry, both the commodities, and the number of the people, fhall be increafed, before they have much commerce with foreign nations to

fetch

fetch them money; in *such* a *condition*, either there *must be* a currency of Paper-credit, or the induſtrious part of the people will be continually obliged to uſe barter, which will expoſe them to many inconveniencies.

IN fact, we ſee that nations have proſpered by ſetting up Banks. This is true of Holland, of Genoa, and of other places *; and it will be found to be true both of England and of Scotland.

BY making the intereſt of money fall, Banks muſt promote induſtry and trade.

PUBLIC Banks are preferable to private Bankers.

IT may be obſerved, that Banks have greateſt credit under free governments, or ſuch as have a mixture of the ariſtocratical or democratical form ; a ſtrong preſumption in their favour. Abſolute monarchies ſeem hardly capable of ſuch a wiſe inſtitution.

* The author in this Eſſay of Banking had chiefly in his view thoſe Banks which had been ſet up in North Britain. And to them alone ſome of his reaſonings can be applied. He had no intention to conſider the different conſtitutions of all the Banks in Europe. However, ſeveral of his obſervations are of a general nature, and may be applied to all Banks whatſoever.

Under

Under arbitrary governments the credit of Banks cannot be firm. Abfolute princes would be difpofed to lay them under contribution, and would have too ready accefs to their treafures. It is eafy to fee, how the ingenious author of the Querift would anfwer the 303d query, which he hath propofed *, " Whether it be poffible for a " national Bank to fubfift and maintain its " credit under a French government?" Perhaps, it might flourifh for a *little time*, under a *very wife* and *juft* prince: but it muft fink under one of another character, who would be tempted to lay hold on its treafures, as our King Charles II. fhut up his exchequer, and feized the money which belonged to his creditors.

In this manner we may better account for the want of Banks and of Paper-credit in France, than by the fuppofition of a fuperior policy in that country, in order to acquire and retain greater quantities of filver and gold. Thus, the French policy in not inftituting Banks, in not admitting fuch a

* Fifth edition, printed 1750.
No man hath explained the general nature of Banking, hath fhown the advantages of Banks, and hath anfwered the objections againft them, more concifely, and with greater force of argument, than this ingenious author ; whofe Querift deferves well to be perufed by every lover of his country, and of mankind.

circu-

circulation of merchants bills as in England, and in not *directly* permitting lending on intereſt, which Mr. Hume imagines to to be a mighty advantage to the French †, appears to be quite the reverſe, and is truly a diſadvantage, ariſing from the pernicious nature of an abſolute monarchy.

However, Banks, like all other political inſtitutions, are attended with inconveniencies. The four following are much inſiſted on.

First; That too great a run may be made upon Banks, and they may not be able to anſwer their notes ; by which many innocent perſons may ſuffer, and a great deal of confuſion may be raiſed in the country. But in anſwer : Though this indeed *is poſſible*, there is *little danger of its happening* ; if the bank is not originally on a bad footing, and the miſmanagements are not very great. Banks have continued long in Europe, without ſuch diſorders ; and may be ſo well conſtituted and managed, as to prevent them in times to come.

Secondly ; It is ſaid, That Banks cannot be depended on during civil wars, or when a foreign enemy is in the heart of the country. But *what* can be preſerved in *ſuch* a caſe ? Shall we make no wiſe eſtabliſh-

† In his Political Diſcourſe of the Balance of Trade.

ments

ments in time of peace,— becaufe we cannot
fecure them in time of war ? 'Tis true, if we
cannot defend ourfelves againft the French
King, or the Pretender, our Banks will be
of little ufe to us.   But, in fuch circumftances, we muft lay our account with greater
loffes than the lofs of our Paper-credit.   We
fhould lofe our more fubftantial riches.   We
fhould lofe our religion and liberty.   In fhort,
we fhould be able to fecure nothing but the
foil of our ifland ; and that too we fhould be
obliged to cultivate, not for ourfelves, but
for others.

Besides thefe objections, which may be
reckoned inconfiderable, there are two of
greater importance.   The one, That Paper-
money prevents the acquifition of greater
quantities of filver and gold.   The other,
That it heightens the price of labour, and
therefore hurts our foreign trade.   But neither of thefe objections refts on a folid foundation.

" Suppose (fays an ingenious writer *)
" there are twelve millions of paper, that
" circulate in a kingdom as money ; and
" fuppofe that the real cafh is eighteen
" millions.   Here is a ftate, which is found

* Mr. Hume in his Political Difcourfe of the Balance
of Trade.

by

" by experience able to hold a ftock of
" thirty millions: I fay, if it be able to hold
" it, it muft of neceffity have acquired it in
" gold and filver, had it not obftructed
" the entrance of thefe metals by this new
" invention of Paper. *Whence would it have*
" *acquired that fum?* From all the king-
" doms of this world. *But why?* Becaufe,
" if you remove thefe twelve millions of pa-
" per, money in this State is below its level
" compared with its neighbours, and it muft
" immediately draw from all of them, till
" it be full and faturate, fo to fpeak, and
" can hold no more." This is the argument
brought to prove that paper-money prevents
the entrance of filver and gold. But it is too
fubtile to be convincing.

If at any period, the coin in any kingdom is eighteen millions, this nation may
carry on a confiderable trade, and in time
may acquire twelve millions more in filver
and gold, without Paper-credit. But if, at
the time at which they have only eighteen
millions in coin, the nation fhould fall into
the ufe of Paper-credit, and fhould circulate
a fum of twelve millions in Paper-money, in
order to quicken induftry, and to enable the
people to carry on a more extenfive trade ;
it is evident, they may carry on a greater
trade with the *thirty* millions of *paper and*
coin,

coin, than with the *eighteen* millions of *coin alone*. And, as they don't take paper in payment from foreign nations, if they are gainers by trade, they muft receive the balance in filver and gold. Confequently, the national ftock muft be fooner increafed in the one cafe than the other. If we fhall fuppofe further, that we could remove the twelve millions of paper-money, without any fhock or confufion; by allowing lefs credit, we would only put a ftop to fo much induftry, and would difable the people from carrying on fo extenfive a trade. This is not the way of bringing in either filver or gold. How is it poffible, therefore, that the want of fo much credit can add to the treafure of the nation in any way whatever?

THE other objection is more plaufible, and is ftated in this manner by Mr. Hume*: " That, by increafing the current fpecies of " a country, we increafe the price of labour " and provifions ; confequently, enable " poorer nations, where labour and provi- " fions are cheaper, to work cheaper, and " underfell us at foreign markets : That this " is even a neceffary confequence of a great " trade, whatever way it is upheld, and is " infeparably connected with great plenty

---

* In his Political Difcourfe of Money.

" of

" of filver and gold.   On which account,
" trade muſt neceſſarily circulate ; and the
" poorer nations muſt gradually carry it off
" from the richer.   However, there is ſome
" confort (it is ſaid) in loſing our trade by
" plenty and fulneſs ; but it is extremely
" fooliſh to loſe it by an imaginary wealth,
" and artificially to increaſe the natural diſ-
" advantages of plenty."

THIS is the moſt plauſible objection, that
ever has been made againſt Paper-credit.
But, when fully examined, it will appear to
be ill founded.

CREDIT of *ſome kind or other* is *neceſſary*
wherever there is much trade.   In nations,
where there is great ſimplicity of manners
and little trade, there is little neceſſity either
of borrowing, or of buying, upon credit.
But as commerce is enlarged, credit muſt be
enlarged in proportion.   There can be little
trade, where every one buys for ready money.

IF therefore we would increaſe our trade,
we muſt ſubmit to the diſadvantages, or rather
natural conſequences,   ariſing from credit ;
ſince credit is *abſolutely neceſſary* to an exten-
ſive commerce.

IN

In whatever manner this credit is given, it may be said to come in the place of money, to answer for it, or to supply the want of it. It may be reckoned money, and is truly a kind of money.

CREDIT can never be given without end. None will give credit but to men of integrity, prudence, and activity, or to men of substance. Here then are *natural* checks and limits, beyond which credit will not be extended.

REGARD being had to these *natural* limits, credit must always be useful to a nation, while it supports and increases industry and useful labour.

BESIDES the credit given by private dealers one to another, and the advantages arising from such credit, equal or greater advantages may be gained by a more regular and public credit, given by Banks under proper regulations, and established by proper authority.

THE credit of these Banks, as well as credit of all other sorts, may be said to create a new species of money; which, like all other kinds of money, must contribute to raise the prices of labour, of provisions, and of

all

all other commodities. But this is neceſſary in commerce, promotes induſtry, and is, upon the whole, a manifeſt advantage.

I T may be granted therefore to Mr. Hume, that Bank-notes contribute to encreaſe the price of labour, and, perhaps, of all ſorts of commodities. But this is not a valid argument againſt banking; ſince it is only by encreaſing *induſtry* and *conſumption*, that bank-notes increaſe theſe prices. Mr. Hume confeſſes, that even a greater quantity of ſilver and gold doth not encreaſe prices immediately; that a certain interval is required, before it produces this effect; that it muſt firſt quicken the diligence of every individual, before it encreaſes the price of labour *. In no other way can bank-notes encreaſe the prices of labour or of goods : Notes muſt, therefore, be beneficial. Nor does any other diſadvantage ariſe from them which doth not ariſe equally from money. It is true, they have no *intrinſic* value ; in which reſpect money is preferable to them. But they are equally uſeful in all kinds of domeſtic commerce. They produce as much induſtry, as is produced by the ſame quantity of money, and ſerve for money in every caſe, except in tranſacting with foreigners.

* In his Political Diſcourſe of Money.

BUT

But might not we have the fame induſtry *without* the notes ? It is abſolutely impoſſible.   As no man can trade to ſo great an extent without credit, as with it ; ſo paper, taken in payments, muſt go farther than money alone.   When a ſpirit of induſtry is once raiſed, it may require a larger circulation of ſpecie to ſupport it, than the gold or ſilver in the country can ſupply.   In this caſe there is an abſolute neceſſity for Paper-credit.   When there are many induſtrious merchants or manufacturers, who could uſefully employ greater ſums than they poſſeſs, or can have on credit from private hands, they can never carry their trade to the utmoſt length, if there is not a *Bank* for furniſhing them with *this neceſſary* credit.   It may therefore be allowed, that Bank-notes raiſe the prices of labour and goods ; but this is not ſo properly the effect of the notes, as of that induſtry which they raiſe and aſſiſt, and which, with all its diſadvantages, is confeſſed to be beneficial to a nation.

Whether in any one year half a million is brought into a commercial country by trade, or iſſued out by Banks, in notes, upon good ſecurity, it will ſerve for the ſame purpoſes.   Part of it will be laid out in producing more of the ſame kinds of commodities which the country produced before ; another

other

other part in making thefe kinds better; another in raifing new manufactures at home; another in procuring more foreign goods. The farmer will raife more and better grain; the grazier breed more and better cattle; the manufacturer make more and better cloth; the artifan make better work, and in a greater quantity; and the merchant will extend his foreign trade. Thus, the notes will propagate and fupport greater induftry; which will do greater fervice, by encreafing the fubftance of a nation, than it can do harm, by raifing the prices of labour and of provifions.

BESIDES; it is not upon the quantity of current fpecie *alone*, that prices depend; they rather depend on the proportion between the number of buyers, and that of fellers. If there are more buyers than fellers, the prices rife, and rife in proportion to the greater number of buyers. When the demand is leffened, or the fellers exceed the buyers, the prices fall; if the demand is much leffened, they fall greatly. Again, this proportion between buyers and fellers depends on a thoufand accidents, that make one fort of goods more neceffary, fafhionable, or faleable, than another. Thus, when money abounds moft, the prices of *fome* things fall very low; and when it is very fcarce, the

prices

prices of *other* things are high.   The moſt neceſſary things, ſuch as corn and cattle, will depend leaſt upon faſhion. Yet theſe depend upon it in *ſome* meaſure.   At ſome times, and in ſome nations, greater quantities of thoſe neceſſary commodities are conſumed than in others.   But corn, and other things that are moſt neceſſary, depend oftner upon worſe and better crops and ſeaſons, and up-on the proportion between the crops of dif-ferent countries.

Besides the quantity of money, the man-ners of the people have a great influence in altering the methods of living, and deter-mining the prices of labour and of commo-dities.   Theſe manners are changeable, and are found very different after long intervals of time.   It is commonly ſaid, that a crown, two or three hundred years ago, ſerved the ſame purpoſes which a pound does at preſent *.   This is true ;   but not always, perhaps, in the ſenſe in which it is common-ly underſtood.   In ſome caſes,   no doubt, one could have purchaſed, for one crown, as much, as he can now purchaſe for four. In other caſes he could not.   But conſider-ing the different methods of living, there is a ſenſe in which it is *always* true.   In thoſe

* Mr. Hume's Political Diſcourſe of Money.

days,

days, in which a quarter of a pound was equivalent to a whole pound at prefent, men *needed lefs* than they do now. They wanted *only* corn, beef, beer, coarfe cloaths and coarfe furniture. A little money purchafed *them.* Men of the fame rank in our days want *finer* cloaths, *finer* furniture; and, *befides* corn, beef, and beer of a *better* kind, they muft have fpiceries, fruits, and wines; and therefore ftand in need of more money to procure them. Thus, the methods of living and men's opinions are conftantly changing; and a variety of circumftances, befides the quantity of current fpecie, contributes to make labour and provifions dearer at one time than at another.

Mr. Hume * feems to be no lefs miftaken in the limits, which he affigns to *trade,* than in his opinion of Banking. According to his maxims, trade gives check to itfelf; and there is a limit, beyond which it *cannot* be encreafed. Poorer nations, that is, nations with lefs money or foreign commerce, can work *cheaper* than thofe, that are richer; and muft, therefore, carry away their trade. On this head, much has been faid of the dearnefs of labour and of provifions in England, of their cheapnefs of France; that the

* In his Political Difcourfe of Money.

French

French can work cheaper by a third.   It is foretold that the French muft gradually carry away the whole foreign trade of England; fince they can underfell the Englifh in foreign markets.

As to this particular fact, that the French work cheaper than the Englifh, I fhall not examine it.   It cannot, however, be true in *all* cafes.   An Englifhman muft, no doubt, be better fed, and earns higher wages *by the day*; but he will work many things *by the piece*, as cheap, or cheaper than a Frenchman.   He works harder, and can do more work in the fame time.   Further, there are places in Britain and Ireland, where provifions are as cheap as in France.   But, be this as it will, and though it fhould be granted, that, in feveral cafes, poorer nations will work cheaper, and be able to underfell thofe that are richer; richer and more commercial nations will, in general, be able to make many things, which poorer nations either cannot make at all, or cannot make fo well. Hence they may maintain a greater foreign trade, notwithftanding a greater quantity of money.   Trade is, indeed, limited, becaufe the earth and every thing in it are limited. One nation can never extend its trade *in infinitum*, or over all the earth.   But a richer nation, by a proper management, may always

ways maintain its superiority in trade over a poorer. Nay, a greater quantity of money or credit, instead of being a loss, will often be an advantage in this view. It will enable richer merchants, both to purchase, and to sell greater quantities of goods; of consequence to purchase and sell them cheaper than poorer merchants. It is not evident either from reason or from experience, that there must be an equilibrium in trade, as in fluids. One may easily account, from other principles, for the circulation of trade, and for its shifting its seat from one nation to another.

But, in truth, neither the riches, nor the happiness of a nation depends so much on foreign trade, as many merchants are apt to imagine. Though such gentlemen are better furnished, than others, with the knowledge of *particular* facts, they are often misled by prejudices, are too confined in their views, and too much consider their own particular traffic. After all that they have asserted concerning the necessity of foreign trade, it may justly be maintained, that such a nation as Britain, with a large territory, may be great and flourishing, may be more powerful than ever it has been hitherto, by industry and domestic commerce, without an extensive foreign trade; since its lands might be so

much

much better cultivated, than they have ever been, and so many new manufactures might be established, as could support, double, nay, perhaps triple, the number of its present inhabitants.

A nation, where the people are not bred to war, but are chiefly employed in agriculture, manufactures, and other arts of peace; if they lye on a continent, where their neighbours have great standing armies, they also must have a standing army, or a very good militia, to defend them from foreign invasions. If they possess an island, such as Britain, and have not a great standing army, or a good militia, they must have as much foreign or domestic trade, as will enable them to support a good navy for their security. Foreign trade is likewise an advantage in other respects. It opens an easy communication with all parts of the globe. It gives us the means of enlarging our knowledge of nature and of mankind, and of acquiring a share of the riches of every nation. If it be managed with wisdom, it may be a more speedy mean of acquiring wealth than domestic commerce alone. If there are no mines in a country, without foreign trade it cannot have either silver or gold. But such an island as Britain, can never be said to depend chiefly on its foreign trade for its
great-

greatnefs and riches. A nation, whofe territory is fo fmall, that its native produce is not fufficient to feed and cloath its inhabitants, cannot fubfift without a foreign trade. The Britifh are in different circumftances. Their ifland is more than fufficient to feed and to cloath its inhabitants, though they were much more numerous than they are. No doubt they will be the better for fome foreign delicacies and ornaments. They will ftand in need of fome foreign materials for improving their domeftic commerce. But thefe can be procured without an *extenfive* foreign trade. If the people be generally induftrious in improving their lands, and in making the beft ufe of the produce of their own ifland, they may both become very numerous, and enjoy the comforts of life in great plenty, with little foreign trade. This is made out by the author of the Querift beyond the poffibility of a reply. This is confeffed by Mr. Hume * ; who acknowledges, that, when induftry and manufactures are once introduced into a nation, they may lofe moft of their foreign trade, and continue, notwithftanding, a great and powerful people. Nay, this gentleman fcruples not to affirm, that the difadvantages to the foreign trade of England, arifing from the high

* In his Political Difcourfe of Commerce.

price

price of labour, are not to be put in competition with the happiness of so many millions of the commons of England, with whose superior riches, above those of any other people, the high price of labour is so closely connected.

SUCH a maxim is suitable to a humane disposition. Agreeably to such a benevolent sentiment, we ought to extend our notions of trade, and consider not only *how much money* it gains to a nation, but how far it is *conducive to the happiness* of the people. That government and policy is best, where most people are most happy and easy. Neither government nor trade ought to be managed with the *sole* view of procuring vast riches to a *few*, at the expence of *grinding* the faces of the poor, and of rendering the labouring people, who are the great body of a nation, miserable. The systems of too many, both merchants and landed gentlemen, tend to no other purpose. While such gentlemen swim in luxury, and *have more than heart could wish*, they grudge a small pittance to the lower classes of mankind. We ought to propose more *equitable* and more *merciful* schemes. By considering things in this light, we may see, how much the policy of England is preferable to that of France.

IT

IT is not propofed to compare the taxes of England with thofe of France, or to determine, which of them are higheft, or impofed with the greateft judgment. When the expences of the French armies and government are fo great, when fuch vaft fums are actually levied, when both the people and their parliaments make fuch loud complaints of their taxes being fo burdenfome, it is fcarce to be conceived, that the difference in the price of labour and of provifions in France and in England fhould arife from the *difference of taxes*. So far as it is real, it arifes from *another* fource. The Englifh *gentry* in general are richer than the gentry in France, excepting thofe of very high rank. The *middling* people in England are richer than thofe of the fame rank in France. The *commons* in France are much poorer, and *live* more poorly, than the commons in England. Riches are *more univerfally* diffufed in England, than in France. Wherever this is to be found, *cæteris paribus*, prices muft be higher. Hence, the difference in the prices of labour and of provifions in France and in England is chiefly owing to the poverty of the commons in France, and to the riches of the commons in England : a truth, which ought to be acknowledged for the honour of Englifh policy. Accordingly, Mr. Hume *

* In his Political Difcourfe of Commerce.

con-

confeffes, that the great advantage of England above any nation at prefent in the
world, or that appears in the records of any
ftory, confifts in the riches of its artifans and
common people ; which, in his efteem, is
moft fuitable to human nature, augments
the power of the State, makes the burden of
taxes feel light on every fhoulder, and ought
to endear to Englifhmen that free government under which they live.   Thus, were
we obliged to make a choice, compaffion,
as well as good policy, might engage us to
prefer a fcheme, by which the *bulk* of a
people will be eafy, to another, that bears
hard upon the *multitude*.   But, in truth,
England may have abundance of foreign
trade, notwithftanding the higher price of
labour.   An extenfive foreign trade is the
natural confequence of a great domeftic commerce ; fince it is fcarce poffible, that an
induftrious nation, confifting of ten millions
of people, fhould not work up many commodities, which they do not want at home,
and fhould not exchange them for the commodities of foreign nations.

P A R T

PART II.

Of National Debts; and of the Source of the National Debts in England.

SECT. I.

Of NATIONAL DEBTS.

THE cafe of public banks and that of public debts feem to be very different. In a commercial nation the inftitution of banks, if not abfolutely neceffary, is, at leaft, of great advantage. As it keeps the money always encreafing, it is calculated, in the nature of the thing, to promote induftry and trade. But public debt can never be profitable in its own nature, tho' it may fometimes be both neceffary, and attended with accidental advantages.

THE cuftom of hoarding up, in the pub-lick treafuries, great fums of money, which prevailed much in ancient times, and is fo
highly

highly applauded by Mr. Hume *, has, at first view, a very specious appearance. It was indeed suited to nations, which, like those of antiquity, lived in simplicity, and had a greater turn to agriculture and pasturage, than to trade †.

If a nation had few commodities or manufactures to export, it was necessary for it to have a good stock of money to purchase corn in times of scarcity. If one, that was chiefly addicted to agriculture, aspired at foreign conquests, it was necessary for it to have great sums of money provided beforehand, in order to enable it to send an army into another country.

Tho such nations may consist of a greater number of people in the same extent of ground, than nations, which have more money, and carry on a greater foreign trade; tho by their labour and industry at home they may have all the conveniencies of life in great abundance; tho they may be more able to defend themselves against an invasion, and may be stronger at home, than a peo-

* In his Political Discourse of Public credit.
† See a Dissertation on the numbers of mankind, in ancient and modern times. Page 95, 96, &c to 104. See also the Appendix to that Dissertation, Page 270, 271, 272.

ple

-ple addicted to trade ; yet they cannot raife fuch great taxes, nor raife them fo eafily and fpeedily, as commercial nations. Confequently, they cannot maintain fuch great armies abroad, and may often be lefs fignificant in the fcale of nations for maintaining the balance of power. They muft, therefore, be extremely frugal. So the Public muft lay up great fums of money for purchafing provifions in times of fcarcity, or for their warlike expeditions, if they refolve not to live on plunder, and to force their fubfiftance wherever they go ; which will often prove a very dangerous experiment.

But nations, which carry on a great trade, and have much money, as they can raife greater taxes more fpeedily, and with lefs burden to the people, are not obliged to the fame rules of frugality. Nay, hoarding up great fums of filver and gold in the public treafury will often be a lofs to the Public. In place of fuch a policy, it will be better if the Government levy no greater taxes than are neceffary for the prefent exigencies of the State, and leave as much money, as poffible, in the hands of the people, to enable them to carry on a more extenfive trade. Hoarding up money in the public treafury is like a private man's locking up

great

great fums in his cheft, which he might lay out to advantage upon intereft, or in trade.

For this reafon, the great quantities of plate, that are faid to be in France in the churches and private houfes, cannot be of any advantage in trade. What neither circulates, nor is a fund of credit, can have no influence in commerce. The French could carry on a much greater trade, if all this plate were circulating. The Britifh too could carry on a greater trade, if every man poffeffed of plate would either employ it in trade, or lend it to fuch as would. In this refpect the Englifh and Dutch, who encourage fervices of china and other earthen ware inftead of fervices of plate, act more in the true fpirit of trade, than the Genoefe. For the fame reafon, the tax on plate can hardly be reckoned impolitic * ; fince, by leffening the quantity of plate, it prevents the want of bullion for the neceffary exigencies of the State. In general, it is both founder and more merciful policy (as Sir Matthew Decker maintains in his Effay on trade) to lay taxes on articles of luxury rather than upon the neceffaries of life.

* Mr. Hume fufpects, that the tax on plate is impolitic in Great Britain. See his Difcourfe on the Balance of trade.

On

On the fame ground, one cannot fee the advantage of fuch banks as Mr. Hume propofes, which lock up all the money, give out paper inftead of it, and never augment the circulating coin *. If there is no other fecret in the bank of Amfterdam, if all thofe vaft treafures, which have been laid up in its dark caverns from time to time, have remained untouched hitherto, it feems to be altogether unfuitable to the policy of fuch a mercantile people †.

After all, a poorer State chiefly addicted to agriculture and pafturage, and lefs employed in procuring the *elegancies and ornaments* of life by an extenfive trade, may be, in many refpects, preferable to a richer commercial nation. The inhabitants of fuch a *poorer* country may be more *numerous*,

---

* In his Political Difcourfe of Money.
The writer of thefe Characteriftics does not mean, that fuch Banks may not be attended with feveral advantages. Undoubtedly, by the circulation of their notes, inftead of the money given in and locked up, commerce may, in fome refpects, be rendered both more eafy, and more fafe. His meaning only is, that thefe, and perhaps other advantages, do not appear to be fo confiderable, as when Banks are authorifed to lend upon good fecurity, either to private perfons, or to the Public.

† The author of the Querift puts a very proper query on this head, " Whether money lying dead in the bank of Amfterdam would not be as ufelefs as in the mine ? 5th edition 1750, query 242.

more

more *healthy*, and more *virtuous*. They may, by being more warlike, be more able to defend themfelves at home; and may like-wife be abundantly provided with the real *neceffaries* and *conveniencies* of life. In fuch circumftances they may adopt every frugal fcheme. They will not need Paper-credit, and but very little money. At the fame time, they may be very *happy*; happier, perhaps, than richer commercial nations. But, if they will not be fatisfied with fim-plicity ; if a people muft have *delicacies* and *ornaments*, and the trade and manufactures that are *neceffary* to procure them ; they muft not exclude thofe maxims, that are fuitable to fuch an end. It is ridiculous to be per-petually extolling trade and manufactures, while we are conftantly railing at what is evidently connected with them, or neceffary to procure them. This is to act inconfiftent-ly, and to aim at impoffibilities.

Taking things in this view, it may be eafily demonftrated, that public debts are not fo difadvantageous in rich commercial nations, as in nations where the agriculture bears a greater proportion to the trade and manu-factures.

A private man may be obliged to borrow, and may borrow with great advantage to his
private

private affairs. The fame thing holds in the cafe of a nation. If the Government has fome grand and ufeful fcheme in view, either to drain marfhes, to render rivers navigable, to encourage fome branches of induftry, or to maintain their liberty or trade againft a powerful and ambitious enemy, and cannot raife the neceffary fums by taxes in due time; it may be prudent to borrow the money, and to eftablifh a proper method of repaying it at leifure *. If the people have confidence in the Government, the fecurities given by the Public, bearing a certain intereft, may not only become a fund of paper-money, which may eafily be transferred from hand to hand, but become *fo convenient* for merchants or others, that they may very reafonably rife above par. Thus there may be a folid foundation for ftocks or public funds. Merchants, having part of their eftates in the ftocks, which they can command at pleafure, may either be *more ready*, than it would be *poffible* for them *otherwife* to be, for any profitable adventure

---

* It is not therefore univerfally true, That a nation ought never to borrow, but always to raife within the year the money neceffary for the current fervice. This is a good general rule; perhaps it ought feldom to be departed from. But, in feveral cafes, it may neither be poffible nor be expedient.

in

in trade ; or, if no such adventure offers, may have a moderate interest for their money. In this there is a manifest advantage. Without doubt, the trade of England has been *promoted*, and its merchants had advantages from the nature of their stocks, above those of other nations *.

* The following queries, proposed by the ingenious Bishop of Cloyne, serve to illustrate the nature of public funds, and shew, that what originally flowed from necessity and want, may afterwards become beneficial to the State.

Query 233. Whether the credit of the public funds be not a mine of Gold to England ? And whether any step, that should lessen this credit, ought not be dreaded ?

Query 234. Whether such credit be not the principal advantage that England hath over France, I may add, over every country in Europe ?

Query 235. Whether by this the Public is not become possessed of the wealth of foreigners, as well as natives : and whether England be not, in some sort, the treasury of Christendom ?

And afterward, treating of the bank of Amsterdam, he asks,

Query 296. Whether it be not the greatest help and spur to commerce, that property can be so readily conveyed, and so well secured by a *compte en banc*, that is, by only writing one man's name for another's in the bank-book ?

Query 297. Whether at the beginning of the last century, those, who had lent money to the Public during the war with Spain, were not satisfied by the sole expedient of placing their names in a *compte en banc*, with liberty to transfer their claims ?

I т

IT is evident likewife, that the fch mes, carried on by the money thus borrowed by the Public and become a part of the National Debts, may fo much *promote the trade and riches* of the nation in certain cafes, that, by a moderate tax upon the additional riches, a fum may be raifed fufficient both to pay the yearly intereft, and gradually to repay the principal.

IT is true, fome moneyed men, who have large fhares in the ftocks, may give over trade, and fatisfy themfelves with the intereft of their money on government-fecurities. This may often be a lofs ; and, when it

Query 298. Whether the example of thefe eafy transfers in the *compte en banc* thus cafually erected, did not tempt other men to become creditors to the Public, in order to profit by the fame fecure and expeditious method of keeping and transferring their wealth.

Query 299. Whether this *compte en banc* hath not proved better than a mine of gold to Amfterdam ?

Query 300. Whether that city may not be faid to owe her greatnefs to the unpromifing accident of her having been in debt more than fhe was able to pay ?

Much to the fame purpofe fays a celebrated French author, fpeaking of England, " It will have a fure " credit, as it will borrow within itfelf, and pay itfelf. " It may happen, that it will undertake enterprizes " above its natural ftrength, and improve againft its " enemies thofe immenfe fictitious riches, which the " confidence repofed in, and nature of its government " will render real."

De l'Efprit des Loix, tome i. *liv.* 19. *chap.* 27.

hap-

happens, I fhall not cavil with any of our writers about a name, and call thefe gentle-men merchants *.   But fuch gentlemen may have got their *money as honeftly*, as others have got their *lands:* they may *ufe* it as *honeftly*, and with *as much advantage* to the public. If fome of them take undue advantages of ri-fing or falling ftocks to gain exorbitant pro-fits, or take undue methods to raife the ftocks; they may not perhaps do more harm than *landed* men by raifing their rents too high, by fqueezing their tenants, by *hoard-ing up* their corn in times of fcarcity, and by grinding the faces of the Poor. *Landed* men ought to be cautious of propofing to abolifh the public debts by a law, or taking away the eftates of the ftock-jobbers, *as idle and ufelefs member of the State.* If ever all *rich, idle, ufelefs* members of the fociety fhould be punifhed, ftockjobbers would not be the *only fufferers.*

IT is not eafy to affign limits, or to de-termine, how far a nation may go in bor-rowing. Neither, indeed, would it be good policy. It is much better to keep far on the fafe fide, and never to *ftretch* the public cre-dit. But, certainly, the limits for fuch a rich commercial nation as Britain, extend

* The writer of the Three Effays refufes to call them merchants.

farther

farther than many have imagined. Dr. Davenant, in the end of the laſt century, when the public debts were about fourteen millions, was poſitive, that, if they were ſuffered to riſe higher, nay, if they were not gradually cleared, England muſt be undone †.

---

† 'Tis in vain for the author of the Three Eſſays (pag. 15, 16.) to pretend, that this prediction has been verified by the change, which has happened in the property of the lands of England ſince the Revolution : A change ſo great, that he imagines a greater would not have happened even after a Turkiſh conqueſt ! 'Tis evident, Davenant had no view to changes of this nature ; he meant, that the lands would be much worſe cultivated, whoever had the property ; that the inhabitants would be greatly diminiſhed, and would become poor. In this ſenſe, which is the true one, the prediction has failed. Davenant was a man of more ſagacity, than to conſider the *change of hands*, and the ſhifting of property, as a certain indication of decline. This is often the ſymptom of the encreaſe of trade and riches (as ſhall be ſhewn afterwards.) It often happens under the beſt and happieſt governments. But, if Britain was to be overrun by a Turkiſh or abſolute Monarch ; if we were to loſe our liberty and free government ; all the miſchiefs that were predicted by Davenant, and many others, would happen. At the ſame time, the property of lands might remain more fixed, than when trade and riches were encreaſing. Hardly, indeed, could there be any cauſe of altering property, but the arbitrary will of the tyrant. The monarch, indeed, might take an eſtate from one of his ſlaves, and beſtow it upon another. But, amidſt the oppreſſions and inſecurity under ſuch a government, we cannot ſuppoſe ſuch a quick encreaſe of riches, as would enable the Induſtrious to purchaſe eſtates ſo faſt, as in times of greater liberty and ſecurity.

Yet

Yet we have feen them rife to thrice that fum, while the nation is become richer than it was before.

However, there muft certainly be a limit: No nation can contract debts without end. Public debts may be too high. One may be authorized to fay, the debts of Britain are *high enough* at prefent; fince the legiflature appears evidently to be of this opinion, and feems anxious to have them reduced.

SECT.

SECT. II.

Of the SOURCE of the NATIONAL DEBTS of England.

WHEN we confider the vaft debts, that have been contracted in England; in one view, it feems impoffible intirely to juftify the conduct, which has been the caufe of them; in another, fuch high debts are not a bad fymptom of the times, and mark a peculiar diftinction betwixt the temper of the nation before and fince the Revolution.

WHEN a free government is able to contract great debts by borrowing from its own fubjects, this is a certain fign, that it has gained *the confidence* of the people. If foreigners are eager to have a fhare of its funds, this fhews the confidence of the *neighbouring nations.* If it be true, that the people of Britain have entrufted the Government with more than fixty millions, and foreigners with more than twenty, fuch a Government muft have *a firm credit.* 'Tis by this firm credit, among other things, that the Government ever fince the Revolution has been remarkably diftinguifhed from the Government during the four preceding reigns.

How

How often have we been told, with a particular emphasis, That all our debts have been contracted since the Revolution? To such, as know the hiftory of former times, the mention of this is unneceffary. None of the four preceding reigns had *any credit* with the people. Before the Revolution the nation could place no confidence in the adminiftration ; for they were continually giving them ground of jealoufy, and were fecretly under-mining, or openly invading, their conftitution.

How openly did James the Firft of England propagate a flavifh fyftem, as the true fyftem of the Britifh government. "The abfolute
" power of kings ; their hereditary, indefea-
" fible, irrefiftable, divine right; the rights of
" their fubjects being originally derived from
" their grace and favour, and being revok-
" able at their pleafure, or in cafes of necef-
" fity, of which they themfelves were the fole
" judges ; their right to levy money at their
" pleafure, and in what manner they found
" moft expedient, without confent of par-
" liament ; their right to prefcribe to the
" confciences of their fubjects, at leaft to re-
" gulate all external forms and ceremonies
" in religion by their fovereign will and au-
" thority ; their right to call members of
" parliament to account, to try, judge, and
" punifh

" punifh them at common law, for their
" fpeeches in parliament :" thefe, and fuch
like flavifh principles, were common topics of his converfation. He inculcated them
upon his courtiers. He talked of them openly at table. He could fcarce conceal them
from his parliaments, and made an affent and
confent to thefe flavifh doctrines the high
road to honour and preferment.

DURING the reign of Charles I. the rights of
the fubjects were fo openly violated, as gave
an univerfal difguft, and made the king lofe
the confidence of his people. Charles himfelf entertained too high an opinion of the
authority of kings. Nor need we be furprifed that the nation was extremely
alarmed, after feeing the court difcover fo
ftrong an inclination to rule without parliaments, and take fuch wide fteps, to eftablifh
an arbitrary government, both in church and
ftate.

WHEN we reflect on the attempts, that
were made againft our freedom during this
reign, we ought not to be ungrateful to the
memory of thofe generous patriots, who, in
oppofition to an arbitrary court, fo bravely
afferted the caufe of liberty, and maintained
the rights of the people. We ought to applaud that valour and love to their country,
which

which fhone confpicuoufly in their character. But as an enormous ambition and enthufiaftic rage at length mixed in their counfels, and hindered them from finifhing happily what they had fo glorioufly begun; in fo far they deferve to be condemned ; nor could they ever obtain a firm credit with the people.

It is needlefs to enter minutely into the fpirit of thofe times. One would not be fond of bringing too fevere an accufation againft the two firft kings of Great Britain. At the fame time, many of their meafures cannot poffibly be defended. Whatever were the virtues of thofe princes as men, as kings they manifeftly aimed at arbitrary power. Whatever were the crimes and weakneffes of thofe who oppofed them, a warm oppofition in thofe two reigns feems to have been neceffary for preferving Britifh liberty. It is extremely difficult to be wholly impartial. Mr. Hume * has not been able to hinder himfelf from fhewing a vifible bias in favour of King Charles I. and of the party who fupported him ; and againft the zealous defenders of civil and religious liberty. It is very poffible, that I am biaffed on the other

* In the Hiftory of Great Britain, vol. I.

fide.

side. The religious Puritans of those days had great weaknesses ; but those weaknesses were more excusable than the superstitious bigotry of Charles's court and ministers. Those who govern ought to be wiser than the people who are governed. In matters of religion, such as have authority ought to shew indulgence to scrupulous consciences. But the court of King Charles I. knew nothing but severity. Contrary both to justice and to good policy, they embroiled the nation for the sake of *some unnecessary ceremonies* in worship. The defenders of civil liberty, no doubt, fell into great excesses, and carried their claims too far. But our historian treats them with a severity not agreeable to that gentleness which he usually exercises towards political mistakes. It is even with caution, according to Mr. Hume, that we ought to ascribe the praises of a good citizen to *Hamden*, tho celebrated by historians of the most *opposite* parties, for virtue and integrity in private life, affability in conversation, penetration and discernment in counsel ; temper, art and eloquence in debate ; industry, vigilance and enterprize in action ; and valour in war *   Nay, so cautious is the historian, that he scruples to determine positively, whe-

* History of Great Britain, vol. I. p. 353.

ther

ther this generous lover of liberty was actuated by private ambition, or by honeft prejudices. How much more generoufly would he have been treated by the nobler antients, who would not have fcrupled to beftow the higheft praifes on his heroic patriotifm, and would have confecrated his name with the Ariftides's, the Brutus's, and the Cato's of the ancient world.

In judging of the merit of ancient parties, it is not equitable to compare *their* principles and manners with thofe of a *more enlightened age*. This is not the fureft way of forming a found judgment of their pretenfions. To do juftice to our brave forefathers, we fhould not compare *their* fpirit and opinions with the opinions and fpirit of *our* times, but with thofe of their cotemporaries and antagonifts. We fhould confider the neceffities to which they were reduced, and what fpirit was fuitable to the age in which they lived. Times of civil war and fierce diffention about religion, notwithftanding the courage and military bravery which they tend to produce, notwithftanding that noble ardor for liberty, and fervent zeal for religion, with which many are remarkably infpired, may juftly be called unfortunate to thofe that live in them. Befides the external calamities of war, with which the world is afflicted

in

in fuch times, they beget an uncommon keennefs, if not acrimony, of temper. We need not, therefore, wonder fo much, as Mr. Hume, that our generous anceftors, who were engaged in fuch arduous conflicts, carried fome things too far; and that their genius, tho fuitable to thofe fierce times in whichProvidence had caft their lot, appears fo different from the milder and more fociable fpirit of the prefent age.

KING Charles II. had reigned but a fhort time after his reftoration, when he loft the confidence of his fubjects. The reftoration of this prince in fo hafty a manner, without fome fuch folemn declarations of the rights of the nation by parliament, as were after-wards made at the Revolution, can be jufti-fied only by the *neceffity* of a fpeedy fettlement at that time. Such an entire confidence was not a little dangerous. The true friends of liberty foon had reafon to repent of their complaifance. This indolent and inactive prince difcovered that he inherited the prin-ciples of his father; tho he would neither run the rifk, nor take the trouble of eftablifh-ing his favourite fyftem. Guided by French and popifh counfels, he foon loft the hearts of his people. How poorly did he fhut up his exchequer, to avoid paying a million and a half of debt, that he might be better able to affift the French to conquer the Dutch, contrary to the intereft of the Nation! What unjuft, fevere, and foolifh attempts were made in his reign, as well as in his father's, to fettle what will always be impoffible to fettle, in a free and proteftant country, an *exact uniformity* in matters of religion! But feverity to proteftant diffenters, and a fecret management in favour of the church of Rome, were prevailing maxims in thofe two reigns.

THE defigns of his fucceffor James II. to eftablifh an arbitrary government, and to reftore popery, were vifible to the whole nation, opened the eyes of the people, and brought about the Revolution.

WHAT confidence could the nation place in princes of fuch characters, who were continually ftruggling with their parliaments, and difcovered a manifeft inclination to be free of them altogether! What *wife* men would have *trufted* fuch princes with their money! None of the four princes before the Revolution had *credit* enough to obtain fuch great fums as the people have chearfully contributed fince that memorable æra.

THIS confidence of the people arifes from the moft obvious and palpable appearances,
and

and is founded on the moſt juſt and reaſonable grounds. Since the Revolution, our princes have avoided thoſe rocks on which their predeceſſors ran with precipitation. The Britiſh have enjoyed greater liberty and ſecurity than were enjoyed in the preceding reigns. The great body of the people find themſelves eaſy and ſafe. The adminiſtration is equitable and mild. The Sovereign ſummons the parliament regularly, according to law. The king and his parliament meet and part amicably. They enact ſuch laws as are thought proper. Sometimes the landed, ſometimes the trading intereſt, is more immediately conſidered. Great regard is paid to the general opinion of merchants and of the people. If they are offended at any law that has been enacted ; if *deſigning* men have raiſed a clamour, and rendered the people uneaſy ; ſuch is the lenity of the Britiſh government, ſuch their regard to the voice of the Public, that, tho the people, perhaps, had no juſt reaſon to have been uneaſy on account of the law itſelf, yet if this law was not thought of importance enough to juſtify the ſuffering them to remain uneaſy under it, it has been known, that, the very next ſeſſion of parliament, the miniſtry have made the motion to repeal it. Inſtead of flagrant attempts to ſtretch the prerogative, as in former times, the people

can

can fee nothing but legal government. If it is doubted, whether the King can execute any particular, neceffary, or falutary project, by virtue of his prerogative, inftead of urging the *plea of neceffity*, as was frequently done before the Revolution, or catching at fuch an opportunity for *enlarging the prerogative* without law; a bill is immediately brought into *parliament* to explain, or to enlarge the powers of the Crown. Amidft affected cries of flavery and oppreffion by the difaffected or difcontented, no body can obferve inftances of this oppreffion. Every induftrious man is able not only to live by his induftry, but to live in much greater plenty, than in France, or under any abfolute monarchy. He finds, indeed, the prices of many things higher, than they were in former times; whether from taxes, or for other reafons, he does not perhaps inquire. Neither does he calculate, how much he pays towards clearing the public debts. But, without any fuch calculation, he finds more money to pay thofe higher prices, and fees that every one may *live happily* under a *gentle* adminiftration, and the protection of law. Such a concurrence of favourable circumftances makes the people eafy. They have *confidence* in the government, and are not to be moved either by the alarms given by the timorous or difcontented, or by the arts of

the

the difaffected, and their ftudied reprefentations of oppreffion and poverty amidft the
greateft liberty and plenty.

But have there been *no* mifmanagements
under the government fince the Revolution ?
Has this government fallen into *no* errors?
Has it been guilty of *no* abufes ? Whatever
may be faid by fawning parafites, the beft
friends of the Revolution will not fay fo.
They do not doubt, that men without virtue, or without ability, have too often been
employed ; that fuch men have mifmanag-
ed public affairs, and embezzled the public money ; that frauds have been committed ; that fervices have been paid for,which
were never performed; that others have
been purchafed at an extravagant price ; that
many deceitful arts have been employed in
the management of the ftocks ; and that
fuch abufes have too feldom been punifhed.
Though they are far from believing that the
balance of power in Europe is an idea *entirely imaginary*, they will not affert, that we
have not burdened ourfelves *too much* to preferve it. Far are they from thinking, that *all*
our foreign wars and negotiations have been
conducted with the *greateft* fkill and ability ;
that our taxes have been impofed with the
deepeft judgment ; that our revenues have
been managed with the *ftricteft frugality*.
They

They cannot believe, that, if the adminiftration fince the Revolution had been entirely patriot and frugal, the public debts
would have rifen fo high, or not have been
fooner reduced. All human governments
are fubject to abufes. The government,
fince the Revolution, has not been exempted
from them. Generous friends of liberty
will not deny it. They will not proftitute
their honour. They will not defend what is
wrong. When they celebrate the government fince the Revolution, they do not celebrate it on account of *the frugality* of the adminiftration, or the watchfulnefs of men in
power, either in preventing or in punifhing
abufes. What they celebrate is of a different nature. By the Revolution the conftitution has been rendered more perfect. That
admirable and fingular mixture of a hereditary limited monarchy and fplendid ariftocracy, without the power of oppreffing, and
of an equal democracy without its unfteadi-
nefs and confufion, fhines with fuperior luftre.
By means of the Revolution, the proteftant
religion, which feemed continually to be in
danger from the influence of popifh kings or
popifh queens, is perfectly fecured. By
means of the Revolution, we enjoy an entire fecurity from all kinds of perfecution,
liberty of worfhipping God according to our
confciences, fafety to our perfons againft arbitrary

bitrary imprifonments, fecurity of our lives and properties from arbitrary judgments, freedom from all taxes, penalties or punifhments, without confent of parliament, liberty of fpeech and debate, of writing and printing, in the moft ample manner we can defire. Thefe are bleffings which we have poffeffed more abundantly than ever we did before. Such perfect liberty and fecurity have given fo great encouragement to induftry and trade, that, notwithftanding our high taxes and great national debts, we are much richer and more powerful, than before the Revolution.

Tho the true friends of liberty will never deny weakneffes in the adminiftration, they cannot but fee, at the fame time, that many of the abufes which they confefs and lament, naturally arife from the freedom of our government, and are evils nearly connected with the bleffings we enjoy above moft other nations. There can be no unmixed happinefs in this world. A nation cannot have *juft enough* of any thing, and no more. If it enjoys a fufficient meafure of liberty, it muft be content to take along with it a certain portion of licentioufnefs. If it will have the *moft perfect* fecurity againft illegal imprifonments or arbitrary judgments, it muft lay its account to fuffer many criminals to efcape.

If

If it would preserve the influence, dignity, and independance of the rich, and not break the spirit of the commons, it cannot expect to be without parties and factions. Where-ever there are struggles and contests for power and authority, *dishonourable* as well as *honourable* methods of acquiring them will too often come into vogue. Where power is divided among many different persons and bodies of men, the distribution is the great mean of preserving freedom, and of preventing those enormous acts of tyranny, which are exercised under absolute monarchies. But it often embarrasses the administration, and makes the springs of government move more flowly. A king of Britain, as he cannot do the thousandth part of the mischief which may easily be done by an absolute monarch, sometimes cannot do so much good. His best intentions may be frustrated by contending parties *. Where there

---

* As it can rarely be supposed, that absolute monarchs will be disposed to do good in any extraordinary degree; as they are surrounded with flatterers from their birth, and their education seldom tends either to give them the largest views of what is best, or best disposes them to pursue it; as they must be often misled, by their courtiers, to prefer other considerations to the general interest of their subjects; as there are indeed but few examples of absolute princes who have been *eminently* good, and every absolute prince is capable of doing the greatest mischief; absolute monarchy always has been, and always must be, the greatest

are

are parties and factions, it is no wonder that persons, whose greatest merit consists in their powerful connexions, are sometimes chosen into offices. No. form of government can have all advantages. The best is that which has the most·and the greatest. If a nation will have moneyed men and rich merchants, who shall be able both to carry on a great trade, and to advance money for the urgent occasions of the government, it must admit stock-jobbing. If it will preserve a due balance of power abroad, and baffle the unjust attempts of an ambitious monarch, who disturbs the peace of mankind, encroaches on his neighbours, and would enslave the world, it must sometimes put itself to the expence of maintaining armies for its defence. If it is more rich and opulent, the administration *must* be more expensive, and must pay all its officers and servants at a much greater rate, than other nations *. Thus we may easily

scourge of mankind. According to Mr. Hume (in his Political Discourse of Commerce) " the poverty of the " common people is a natural, if not an infallible, " consequence of absolute monarchy." In this view, it is the best policy for nations to set proper bounds to the power of their kings. This the British have happily effected, and have established the wisest monarchy that ever was in the world.

* Mr. Hume has observed (in his Political Discourse of Money) that all rich trading countries, from Carthage to Britain and Holland, have made use of mercenary troops ; that the pay of all servants in rich countries must rise in proportion to the public opulence ;

see

fee the original fource of many abufes, that are juftly complained of.

" King William's wars! King Wil-" liam's wars!"——A great topic of declamation to fuch as are difaffected. It muft be owned, that it is fcarce poffible, without knowing many fecret tranfact ons, to explain the reafons, and to fhew the neceffity of foreign wars. But thofe entered into by King William immediately after the Revolution, and that projected by him a little before his death, as far as the Public can judge, feem to have been undertaken upon the moft honourable occafion *. It was *glorious* for the nation to chaftife the pride of an ambitious monarch, who had affifted King James with his fleets and armies, and, like a defpotic mafter, would force the Britifh to fubmit to a Prince whom they had

and that our fmall army in Britain of twenty thoufand men is maintained at as great expence, as a French army thrice as numerous. Therefore, according to this writer, we ought not to expect to be as frugal as the French, till the commons of England fhall be as poor as thofe of France.

* We find a very abfurd affertion (in the Three Effays, page 11.) That it is the intereft of landed men and merchants to fubmit to any infult, rather than engage in a war; fince they muft bear the whole burden of it.

pro-

profcribed †. It was *generous* to make an atonement to Europe for the weakneffes of Charles II. not only in fuffering, but in affifting, the haughty Lewis to trample on the faith of treaties, and on the rights of nations. It was *neceffary* for their own intereft, to join their arms with the reft of Europe, which the encroachments of Lewis XIV. had at length roufed to take juft vengeance, and to concert proper meafures for their own fecurity.

But it cannot be expected, that the flatterers of a tyrannical Power in Church or State will ever be reconciled to the memory of William III. How glorious is it for him, that he was fo much hated by them while alive, and that his memory has been fo much perfecuted fince his death! Even the elegant Monfieur de Voltaire, poffeffed of as much freedom of thought as is to be obferved in any writer born under an abfolute monarchy, is far from doing juftice to this great man.

† This is the language of Monfieur Voltaire : Mais reconnaitre ainfi pour leur roi un prince profcrit par eux, leur parut un outrage à la nation, & un defpotifme qu'on voulait exercer dans l'Europe. *Siecle de Louis* XIV. tome i. chap. 16.

Ac-

ACCORDING to Monſieur Voltaire *, King William III. was more remarkable for depth of judgment, than beauty of genius or force of imagination. In his manners he was plain and modeſt, uſually grave and re-ſerved, and never lively but in a day of bat-tle. He deſpiſed all kinds of ſuperſtition, and never perſecuted any perſon on account of Religion. He had the valour of a ſol-dier, and reſources of a commander; and, tho he loſt many battles, left behind him the reputation of a General much to be dreaded. He had an abſolute influence in Holland, but did not deſtroy its liberty: Nor had he any *inclination* to render himſelf abſolute in England. Without being po-pular he was a great politician; and was, indeed, the ſoul and prime mover of the half of Europe. Hitherto this Hiſtorian ſeems diſpoſed to do juſtice. In what fol-lows his good diſpoſition towards this great prince is not ſo conſpicuous. He died (ſays he) without giving any anſwers to what the Engliſh Clergy ſaid to him about their re-ligion, and diſcovered no anxiety about any thing but the affairs of Europe. If Mr. Voltaire intended this as a tacit accuſation of impiety, it is ſcarce pardonable in an author who affects ſo much to deſpiſe *ſuper-*

* Siecle de Louis XIV. chap. 16.

ſtition.

ftition. He has likewife palpably miftaken the character of King William, and put an unjuft glofs upon the referve that appeared in the laft fcene of his life. This hero affected not fhew or popularity during his life : he had too great a foul to alter his manner, and to affect them at his death. Having often faced death in the field with courage, he felt its actual approaches without any concern for himfelf, and had no other concern but for the welfare of Europe.

To judge of him from his actions, and to put the moft natural conftruction on his conduct, the welfare of Europe, and the prefervation of liberty, were always in his view ; the accomplifhment of thefe great ends the main bufinefs of his life.

According to M. Voltaire, the Prince of Orange had conceived vaft defigns, nay, was more ambitious than Lewis XIV. This may be allowed. There are few great men without great ambition. But the ambition of Lewis and that of William were entirely different. Lewis was ambitious of rendering his power abfolute at home, and of deftroying any remainder of liberty that was to be found in France : William was ambitious of preferving the rights and liberty
of

of his country. Lewis was ambitious of fubduing and enflaving all the neighbouring nations : William of protecting them againft the attacks of Lewis. Lewis attacked Holland from pride and a defire of glory : It was the glory of William to defend that finking State. Lewis was ambitious of deftroying the proteftant religion in France : William, of protecting and preferving it in Britain. Lewis was ambitious of making confcience yield to his defpotic fway : William, of preferving the rights of confcience facred and inviolable. Lewis's ambition was accompanied with *injuftice and cruelty*, both to his own fubjects and to his neighbours : William's, with *juftice and mercy*. To finifh the comparifon : Lewis was difappointed of his ambitious purpofe to eftablifh an univerfal monarchy : William fucceeded in his great defign of humbling tyrants. William in his life fet bounds to the power of Lewis, and ftopped the career of his conquefts. By the execution of the fchemes which William had projected while alive, even after his death he brought down the high fpirits of Lewis, and fpoiled him of his former trophies.

IT is difficult even for men of liberal minds wholly to diveft themfelves of the prejudices of education. M. Voltaire is a

ftrik-

ftriking proof of the truth of the obfervation. Tho he allows, that King James's
going over to France at the Revolution was
the æra of the true liberty of England * ;
that the wars which King William projected and Queen Anne profecuted, were in
reality the wifhes of the nation † ; that
Lewis XIV. had taken up arms himfelf
againft his own nephew, againft his fon's
brother-in-law, and againft another prince
nearly allied to his family ; that the Duke
of Savoy fought againft the hufband of one
of his daughters, and againft the father-in-
law of the other : yet, paffing over thefe
examples of ambition in thofe two princes
with a gentle cenfure, he attacks the Prince
of Orange moft unjuftly, in a manner truly
abufive, and altogether unworthy of the
fine fenfe and penetration of fuch an ingenious hiftoriographer.

" The moft criminal undertaking in all
" that war, was the only one that was truly
" fuccefsful. William fucceeded entirely
" in England and Ireland : in other re-
" fpects fuccefs was balanced by loffes.

* Ce fut là l'époque de la vraie liberté d' Angleterre. *Le Siecle de Louis* XIV. tome i. chap. 14.

† L.s mefures étaient les vœux de la nation. *Le
Siecle de Louis* XIV. tome i. chap. 16.

" When

" When I call this undertaking criminal,
" I do not examine, whether the Britifh,
" after having fhed the father's blood, were
" in the wrong, or had juft reafons, to
" banifh the fon, and to defend their reli-
" gion and their rights : I only fay, that,
" if there is fuch a thing as juftice upon
" earth, it did not belong to the daughter
" and fon-in-law of King James to turn
" him out of his own houfe *. "

Seldom has Mr. Voltaire fuffered fuch an exceptionable paragraph to drop from his pen, or treated his fubject fo fuperficially. The daughter and fon-in-law of King James were not either unjuft or criminal in giving a feafonable affiftance to Great Britain againft the unlawful attempts of that prince. The rights of kings and of their heirs, and all the rules of fucceffion, muft

---

* L'entreprife la plus criminelle de toute cette guerre, fut la feule veritablement heureufe. Guillaume reüffit toujours pleinement en Angleterre & en Irlande. Ailleurs les fuccès furent balancés. Quand j'appelle cette enterprife criminelle, je n' examine pas fi la nation, après avoir repandu le fang du pere, avait tort au raifon de profcrire le fils, & de defendre fa religion & fes droits : Je dis feulement, que s'il y a quelque juftice fur la terre, il n'appertenait pas à la fille & au gendre du Roi Jâques de le chaffer de fa maifon. *Le Siecle de Louis* XIV. tome i. chap. 15.

ever

ever be fubjected to the general good and exigencies of nations. No race of kings can juftly lay claim to an unalterable right of fucceffion in all events, and upon all fuppofitions whatever. The rights of nations and the authority of laws are fuperior to the rights and authority of kings. Notwithftanding the *ftrongeft ties* of gratitude and *natural relation* to any king, it will ever be juft and glorious to deliver an oppreffed nation, and refcue a finking State from tyrannical power. Neither humanity, nor gratitude, nor natural affection, can bind up any of his family from defeating his unjuft and deftructive fchemes fubverfive of the happinefs of a whole people. If open force be neceffary for this good purpofe, the neceffity renders it lawful. Gratitude and natural affection can oblige to nothing more, than treating the perfon and family of the Prince with due tendernefs and refpect. This was abundantly taken care of at the Revolution. The Prince of Orange at all times fhewed as much regard for King James, as filial piety demanded; and, on certain delicate occafions, treated him with a generofity which marked the greatnefs as well as goodnefs of his mind. M. Voltaire has been blinded by his prepoffeffions. Tho he was able to overcome the prejudices he had contracted in favour of a fuperftitious religion, he has

not

not been able thoroughly to perceive the odiousness of tyranny, nor divest himself of an admiration of absolute power. So fatal is it to have been born under a despotic prince. Had M. Voltaire written with as much taste and impartiality on this, as on many other subjects, instead of condemning the Revolution, or accusing the Prince of Orange of injustice, he would have fallen down and worshipped, and taught the wondering world to revere that Liberty, which shone so brightly on Britain at that happy period, and was so little known among the neighbouring nations.

But it is less surprising, that a Frenchman, who *professes* himself an admirer of what the author of a late Estimate * calls the gallant reign of Lewis XIV. should be less favourable to the memory of that hero, who defeated the designs of his favourite monarch. We may indeed wonder that the author of the Estimate, who hath enjoyed the blessings of British liberty, should not, even when he confesses that the people of Britain gained an accession of liberty, and British parliaments a new dignity and power, by the Revolution, place the happy instru-

* An Estimate of the Manners and Principles of the Times, p. 138.

ment

ment of thofe valuable acquifitions in a fairer light, and reprefent his conduct in brighter colours. The deliverer of Britain from popery and arbitrary power is not celebrated for wifdom in counfel, bravery in war, hatred of tyranny, or love of liberty; but, in the *Eftimate*, appears in the obfcure light of an *election-jobber*, diftributing places and penfions, in order to the *making of parliaments*.

WILLIAM III. fays he, found an eager defire, in members of parliament, to obtain lucrative employments in exchange for their concurrence in granting fupplies and forwarding the meafures of government, to be the national turn; and fet himfelf, like a politician, to oppofe it. He therefore filenced all he could by places or penfions: And hence the *origin* of making of parliaments *.

I WILL not fay, that every author is obliged to write panegyrics, or to celebrate even the greateft heroes. But no author has a right to be *unjuft* to any man whom he introduces in his writings: neither is it lawful to impute to him errors or crimes with which he is not chargeable.

* Eftimate, page 109.

I DO

I do not inquire, how far the practice of *silencing* all, who laid claim to lucrative employments, by places or pensions, obtained in the reign of King William. I abhor bribery in all its shapes, and condemn the minister, who offers a bribe to any member of parliament to vote against his conscience. If he offers the bribe to engage him to vote according to his conscience, I will not make an apology for him *. Offering bribes, in any case, is criminal in its own nature ; nor can the end sanctify the means. I do not vindicate that measure, which was approved even by the austere Cato, who thought it lawful to foil Cæsar at his own weapons, and, in order to defeat his wicked designs, to offer a greater bribe, than was offered by the tyrant †. But, whatever danger may be conceived from the practice of making parliaments, or from attempts of this kind, if it was intended by the author of the Estimate to fix the æra of the commencement of this practice at the Revolution, or to ascribe the origin of it to King William III. he is altogether mistaken. It is true, the four princes of the House of Stewart were not fond of Parliaments. They often endeavoured to

* Estimate, pag 114, 115.
† Sueton. in Jul. Cæf.

govern without them. But when they found it neceffary to have recourfe to them, they fpared neither coft nor intrigue, both to influence the elections of members, and to gain them to their meafures after they were elected; and thus ufed great efforts to make parliaments. Did not Charles I try to break the party that had been formed againft his meafures, by conferring honours and lucrative offices on the chief men in the oppofition? In Charles II's reign, the names and prices of the penfioners of the Court were publicly known. Did not James II. clofet members of parliament, and ufe all forts of arts to gain a parliament to favour his defigns?

It can fcarce be imagined, the author of the Eftimate cou'd be ignorant of all this. I will not fuppofe, that he intended to afcribe the origin of the pernicious policy of attempting to make parliaments, to the great King William.

It is juftice to put the moft favourable fenfe upon the words of a writer. If thofe, ufed by the author of the Eftimate, are capable of this fenfe, I will fuppofe he intended them in honour to King William, and meant no more, than that whatever *endeavours* had been formerly ufed to make

par-

parliaments, yet parliaments had never *actually* been made till the reign of King William * Thus much at leaft muft be granted, if we will ufe the ungracious and unconftitutional phrafe of making parliaments, That, during the four reigns preceding the Revolution, parliaments could feldom be made, and were therefore fo of-

* The Author of the Eftimate, in his fecond Volume page 193, gives an explanation of the Paffage in the following words, " That the practice of making Parliaments was now, (that is in the reign of " William the third) firft laid down as a neceffary " Principle of Government ;" and this, according to him, " was the neceffary confequence of leffening the " Prerogative, where Parliaments were felfifh " But this explanation would, perhaps, itfelf require an additional remark. For this practice was not laid down, either at that or any other time, by any open and avowed declaration of any man or body of men. And in fo far as it was *refolved upon* by any minifter, it was not, in this fenfe, *firft* laid down after the Revolution. It had been laid down by many minifters in former periods. 'Tis true, that they laid down *other* rules, which have been *difcontinued* fince the Revolution. When they could not gain their end by the diftribution of places and of penfions, they made ufe of arbitrary and violent means, which caufed great diftractions in the nation. Yet it may charitably be allowed, that few of our former minifters had recourfe to thefe arbitrary methods, till they had tried the *other* to the utmoft of their power, and had found themfelves unfuccefsful thro the jealoufies of the people. If it is meant, that it muft have been laid down by tacit confent, and that fince the Revolution it was

ten

ten haftily diffolved. During thefe reigns, both the parliaments and the people entertained jealoufies of their kings. Thofe jealoufies, for which their conduct had given too much ground, put it out of *their* power to *make parliaments*. It has only been fince the Revolution, after the nation had fecured their rights in the moft folid and ample manner, and there was no longer any apprehenfion of popery and arbitrary power, that there has been fo good a correfpondence between our princes and their parliaments.

It is true, this good correfpondence has often been afcribed to other caufes, that are not fo honourable. Much has been faid of bribery and corruption. He would defervedly be laughed at, who would not allow that a great deal of it is true. He is no a good citizen who does not lament it fincerely. However, one may be a good citizen, and yet think better of his country-

more neceffary, and therefore more practifed, than formerly ; neither can this be proved, till it is firft p oved, that under fuch a Government, as we have had fince the Revolution, the nation either has been, or ought to have been, as jealous of their princes ; or that the meafures of the Government have been, or ought to have been, as unacceptable to the body of the people ; or that this government has been as unwilling, as the former, to abandon meafures, which appeared generally difagreeable.

men,

men, than the author of the Eſtimate. It may be unpopular, perhaps, it may be reckoned bold, to aſſert it ; but it is hoped, it will be found to be true, That it is not in the power of any miniſtry, in the preſent times, by the higheſt offers, to bribe either the repreſentatives or their conſtituents to part *with the rights*, and give up the *conſtitution*, of their country. " A gift blind- " eth the wiſe, and perverteth the words of " the righteous *. " Places and penſions will have too much influence : yet we have great reaſon to hope, that, if a trial were to be made, a majority would be found to aſſert the dignity of our parliaments, and the liberty of our people.

No doubt, we may often be too laviſh of our money, and not ſufficiently attentive to the public intereſts. Inſtead of giving check to raſh and forward miniſters, who would fooliſhly engage us in unneceſſary quarrels ; inſtead of chaſtiſing indolent and puſilanimous miniſters, who neglect the honour of their king and the ſafety of their country ; we may ſometimes be lulled aſleep, and miſled by miniſterial arts. But, notwithſtanding the effeminacy and venality of our times, it is greatly to be hoped, that, *upon equal*

* Exodus xxiii. 8.

provo-

provocation, both our parliaments and people would be as untractable as before the Revolution ; that having been accuſtomed during ſeventy years to ſo glorious a liberty, we would endure the greateſt hardſhips, rather than part with it ; and that the poſterity of thoſe heroes, who brought about the Revolution, will not look either upon it, or upon the happy inſtrument who ſo greatly conducted it, as the ſource and origin of their preſent corruption ; but will conſider the ſettlement made at the Revolution as the great charter of their freedom, and the heroic prince who conducted it as raiſed up by Providence for the good of mankind, and the defence of injured nations.

IT is much in this light the ingenious Mr. Hume has conſidered the Prince of Orange, and the eſtabliſhment at the Revolution. For, tho no body will accuſe him of being prejudiced againſt the princes of the houſe of Stewart, he allows, That the fluctuation and conteſt of the Engliſh government were, during the four reigns preceding the Revolution, much too violent both for the repoſe and ſafety of the people : That foreign affairs at that time were either entirely neglected, or managed to pernicious purpoſes : That, in the domeſtic adminiſtration, there was felt a continual fever, either ſecret or manifeſt,

manifeſt, ſometimes the moſt furious convulſions and diſorders : That the Revolution forms a new epoch in the conſtitution, and was attended with conſequences much more advantageous to the people, than the barely freeing them from bad adminiſtration. And tho he ſcruples to determine, whether we in this iſland have ever ſince the Revolution enjoyed the *beſt ſyſtem of government*, he affirms in the ſtrongeſt manner, that we have enjoyed the moſt entire *ſyſtem of liberty*, that ever was known amongſt mankind *.

As to the Prince of Orange, who condɔ́ted this great undertaking, tho our hiſtorian will not prefer his virtue to that of Ariſtides, Leonidas, Epaminondas, Pelopidas, Timoleon, the Catos, the Brutuſes, Marcus Aurelius Antoninus, and all the other heroes, whoſe virtues have been recorded in the annals of hiſtory, he has, however, erected a very noble monument to his glory. " The prince of Orange, he ſays, through-
" out his whole life, was peculiarly happy
" in the ſituation in which he was placed.
" He ſaved his own country from ruin. He
" reſtored the liberty of theſe kingdoms
" (Britain and Ireland.) He ſupported the
" general independency of Europe. And

* Hiſtory of Great Britain, vol. II. pag. 443.

" thus

" thus—it will be difficult to find any per-
" fon, whofe actions and conduct have con-
" tributed more eminently to the general
" interefts of fociety and mankind *."

Thus our lateft Hiftorian, more than fifty years after the death of this prince, has contributed to render his memory and the memory of the Revolution immortal. In truth, the Revolution, and the fettlement of the government that was made at that time, was one of the beft conducted enterprifes, one of the moft important events, one of the moft beneficent tranfactions, and, finally, one of the moft folemn, deliberate, juft, and prudent eftablifhments of government, that perhaps ever happened in the world. And, among all the great men, who have been famous in later ages, it will be difficult to name one, who had *greater virtues* and *fewer weakneffes* than King William III.

But there is no unmixed happinefs on earth. Every thing is attended with dif-advantages. Britons have been put to con-fiderable expence to fupport the Revolution. No fooner had the happy change been made, than we were obliged to defend what we

* Hiftory of Great Britain, vol. II. pag. 420, 421.

had

had fo bravely atchieved againft the power of Lewis XIV. who would have reftored King James. After the death of King William, Lewis, contrary to the faith of treaties, acknowledged the Pretender to be King of Britain. Such an outrageous affront, offered to the King and kingdom, according to the accounts given to Mr. Voltaire *, effectually roufed the Britifh nation to arms, and kindled another war. Both thefe wars were expenfive, and involved the nation in debt : but they were no lefs neceffary for our fecurity againft the power of France, than for the fupport of the Revolution. The negligence and bad policy of Charles II. had fuffered the power of France to become dangerous to all Europe. It was neceffary for Great Britain to enter into meafures with the States on the continent, to curb this exorbitant power. This put us to expence. Nor muft we grudge neceffary expence of this kind, till the formidable power of France fhall be broken, and that kingdom be brought down to the level of the neighbouring nations. This might have been happily accomplifhed in the reign of Queen Anne, had the negotiations for peace been as wifely and as nobly conducted, as the operations of the

* Le Siecle de Louis XIV. tome I. chap. 16.

war

war had been magnanimous and successful. But, unfortunately, that opportunity was lost. May the present be more wisely improved, and to the honour of his present Majesty! If the French do not yield to every thing necessary for our safety, may he humble the pride of France in a war by sea, that shall be more glorious and successful, than any land-war under the greatest of his predecessors!

IF we reflect on the ambitious spirit of the French Government for more than an hundred years past, we need not wonder, that we have been obliged to maintain expensive wars against so enterprising a nation. Had the Government avoided such wars altogether to save a present expence, had they remained stupidly unconcerned about the interest of their country and that of Europe, or had they, like King Charles II. favoured the ambition, and promoted the dangerous designs, of France; they had acted both ingloriously and unwisely. But their efforts, notwithstanding the narrow conceptions of such as would debar us from intermeddling in the affairs of the continent, must tend greatly to their honour. However, it is far from my intention to enter into any question about particular engagements, or to assert, that several unnecessary expences have not

been

been incurred during our late wars againſt France.

BESIDES the wars in which the nation has been engaged againſt a foreign power, we have been laid under the diſagreeable neceſſity of defending our conſtitution againſt the diſaffected at home, who have never been able to overcome the prejudices of education, and to diveſt themſelves even of the moſt ridiculous and abſurd principles which had been taught them by their parents, or had been the diſtinguiſhing tenets of thoſe parties in which they had been early engaged. It is to theſe early prejudices, it is to miſtaken notions of loyalty, and of the reverence due to government, and not to any wicked intention, one would wiſh to impute the oppoſition that has been made to the Government ſince the Revolution. " As mere nonſenſe " as paſſive obedience ſeemed (ſays the noble " author of the Characteriſtics) we found it " to be the common ſenſe of a great party " among ourſelves, a greater party in Eu- " rope, and, perhaps, the greateſt part of " all the world beſide *." We need not wonder, therefore, that ſuch paſſive principles, notwithſtanding all their abſurdities,

* Eſſay upon the Freedom of Wit and Humour.

ſhould

fhould have taken fo deep root, if we reflect
on the pains that were taken to propagate
them, during the reigns of four fucceffive
princes, who ufed their moft ftrenuous endeavours to eftablifh this paffive fyftem, and
both ridiculed and perfecuted the patrons of
free government.

BUT, tho we can make allowances for the
weakneffes of mankind, we cannot help condemning their erroneous and dangerous fyftems of government. We cannot but be
forry, that they are fo much deluded, and
that there are, among Britons, fome, who,
like the Cappadocians of old *, have refuf-
ed

* Juftin. lib. xxxviii. cap. 2. His words are, " Sed
" Cappadoces, munus libertatis abnuentes, negant vi-
" vere gentem fine rege poffe."
As the Ancients had not a clear idea of a limited monarchy of the beft kind, nor had ever feen fuch a government as the Britifh, under King, Lords, and Commons, they looked upon the government of kings as
oppofite to a ftate of liberty. Where kings are arbitrary, or, as Juftin expreffes it (fpeaking of the moft
early kings, lib. i. cap. 1.) " Populus nullis egibus
" tenebatur: arbitria principum pro legibus erant,"
the oppofition is moft juft; but where the king is limited, as in Great Britain, there is more liberty and
fecurity, than under any other kind of government
whatfoever. It can hardly indeed be denied, that an
ariftocracy, or a democracy, where mankind are more
upon a level, is better calculated to encourage genius
and activity, than any monarchy whatfoever. But this
advan-

ed to be free, and account themfelves un-worthy of that liberty, which was fo brave-ly purchafed at the Revolution. Nay, but we *will* have a king *, fay they, an abfolute, uncontroulable, irrefiftable king, and will be

advantage is more than counterbalanced by the danger-ous factions which naturally arife under fuch conftitu-tions. It may fafely be affirmed, that perfons of all degrees enjoy more liberty and fecurity under the Bri-tifh monarchy, than perfons of the fame rank enjoyed under the Athenian, Roman, or any other of the ancient ariftocracies or republics. For this reafon, the cele-brated Montefquieu, many of whofe principles concern-ing government are not only more juft and noble than thofe of his countrymen, but worthy of a free man; and fhew, how well he underftood, and how greatly he admired the Britifh conftitution; had good ground (in his De l'Efprit des Loix, liv. xi. chap. 6.) to fay, that Har-rington had fearched for liberty, after having over-looked it, and that he had built Chalcedon, having the coaft of Byzantium before his eyes. The plan formed by Harrington is one of the beft models of a *republic*, that was ever conceived. Could we fuppofe it once fully eftablifhed in a *virtuous* age and nation, it might laft long, and feems to have few principles of diffolu-tion. But Harrington erred in imagining that fuch a republic could have been either erected or preferved in the age and nation for which it was projected. Such a perfect republic requires a higher degree of virtue, than is now to be found amongft any of the nations with which we are acquainted. The *limited monarchy* of Great Britain feems to be the moft perfect government of which mankind are capable in the prefent condition of the world. Of Britain it may be faid, no lefs than of Cappadocia, but much more to the honour of Britain, " Vivere gentem fine rege non poffe."

* Firft Book of Samuel, chap. viii. ver. 11—20.

as

as much enflaved as the French or any of the neighbouring nations. In oppofition to all fuch flavifh refolutions, we will affert our liberty : and, as we muft impute a confiderable part of our debts to the neceffity we have been laid under of defending it againft the fecret plots and open attacks of the difaffected, we muft look upon *them* as accountable for no fmall part of the expence of the Government in fupport of the Revolution, notwithftanding their loud complaints againft thefe very expences.

How fatally miftaken are thofe deluded afferters of the hereditary indefeafible rights of kings, and of their abfolute, irrefiftable, uncontroulable power over their fubjects. How ungenerous is it, as well as unjuft and contrary to good policy, in any of the people of Britain to rebel againft the fettlement made at the Revolution, or the family now reigning : a family which, without having ufed any influence whatfoever to obtain the crown, has been called, in a cafe of neceffity, by the choice of the nation, to take poffeffion of it, in order to defend the civil and religious rights of the people of Great-Britain: a family, which fucceeds to the Crown as the neareft heirs of our ancient princes, after the *juft and neceffary exclufion of the Popifh* line : a family, which, during the fpace
of

of forty years, since its acceffion to the throne, has governed *entirely* according to law : a family, under which this ifland has been greatly enriched *, and which is now fo firmly eftablifhed upon the throne.

GENEROUS men will be far from infu'ting the misfortunes of any family whatever. They will not rejoice in their calamities, even when thefe calamities have been brought upon them by their own mifmanagement. They will difdain to aggravate their weak-neffes, or mifreprefent any of their defcendants. But, for the fake of truth, from the love of juftice, from a regard to the dignity of our parliaments, and to the rights and liberties of the people of Great Britain, they muft be fuffered to put the queftion, What family would the difaffected in this ifland fet up in oppofition to the juft and merciful princes of the family on the throne? Do not the family, to which they are fo fatally devoted, affert their abfolute, indefeafible title to our fubjection, independent on any choice, or confent, or advantage of ours ? Do not they affert, that they are accountable to none but God and their priefts, for the injuftice they may exercife towards their fubjects? Do not they maintain, that they ought not

* This fhall be proved afterwards.

to be refifted upon any pretence whatſoever ?
What more ample dominion could one lay
claim to over his cattle ? By their education
muſt they not have contracted an averſion
to Britiſh liberty, conceived high notions of
the abſolute power of kings, and learned an
abject ſubmiſſion to the maxims, and a deep
reverence for the ſuperſtition, of the church of
Rome ? Inſtead of endeavouring to gain the
favour of the Britiſh nation, and recommend
themſelves to our regard, have they not choſen, even ſince the rebellion in the year
1745, to be more cloſely connected than
formerly with the Pope and conclave, by
ſuffering one of their ſons to become a Cardinal ? an inſtance of bigotry, or contempt
of Britiſh Proteſtants, ſcarce to be paralleled,
and ſuch an extraordinary piece of policy *
as can hardly be interpreted otherwiſe, than
as a ſign of their deſpairing ever to make
good their claim to the Crown of Britain ;
or, if they can be ſuppoſed not to deſpair,
as bidding defiance to all Britiſh Proteſtants,
and declaring how much they deſpiſe any
oppoſition that can come from the Britiſh

* According to the principles of an hereditary, in-
defeaſible right of a family to a throne, and agreeably
to the forms of the Church of Rome, Cardinal Stewart
may be choſen Pope, and, upon the death of his father
and brother, and their heirs, may become heir to the
Crown of Great Britain.

nation.

nation. This is the family the difaffected would fet upon the throne. But what ought not a brave and wife Proteftant nation to expend in defending the Proteftant religion, and the freedom of their government, againft the efforts of fuch a family * ? Liberty can never be bought too dear.

* This nation (fays a celebrated French author, fpeaking of England) will love its liberty prodigioufly, becaufe this liberty will be real ; and it may happen, that, to defend it, its people will facrifice their money, their eafe, their interefts; that they will burden themfelves with taxes the moft grievous, and fuch as a defpotic prince would never dare to impofe upon his fubjeas. *De l'Efprit des Loix,* tome I. liv. 19. chap. 27.

PART

PART III.

Of National Riches; and of the Riches of Great Britain.

SECT. I.

Of National Riches *in general.*

A Nation may be opulent and flourishing at the fame time that public debts are high. This will appear to be the condition of Britain at prefent. It is capable of a very clear proof, and is a fubject worthy of our confideration.

In our inquiries concerning wealth, it is ufual to confider filver and gold as the moft fubftantial riches, as well as the moft neceffary means of procuring them : but neither the one, nor the other, is true. *Induftry* is the *chief mean* of acquiring riches :

It

It is far more neceffary than filver or gold·
The moft fubftantial riches confift in the
abundance of thofe things which are neceffary for the fupport and comfort of life.
Where thefe are in plenty, it is of little confequence what the money or the bullion is,
or whether there is any money or not.
Money ferves only for an eafier exchange of
commodities, and to fix their various values
in proportion to one another. In this refpect
it is *ufeful.* It may alfo be confidered as *real*
wealth; both becaufe the precious metals
have a *certain intrinfic* value, and becaufe
mankind have agreed to ufe them as a common ftandard. But, compared with the
cattle, corn, and other commodities, money
is certainly a trifle *.

SUPPOSE each man in the nation had 3 *l.*
in cafh, and there were ten millions of people, we would have thirty millions of coin;
a greater fum, perhaps, than is abfolutely
neceffary for our ommerce. Yet how
fmall a proportion do thirty millions bear
to the whole value of the lands, and

* Dr. Davenant, who wrote many pieces on Political Arithmetic in the end of the laft century; the
Bifhop of Cloyne, in his Querift; and Mr. Hume, in
his Political Difcourfes, agree in this opinion about
money.

all

all the other wealth of Britain and Ireland!

SUPPOSING, again, that, at any one point of time, every man loſt all the caſh in his cuſtody; how ſmall a part of their real ſubſtance would be loſt by the generality either of the poor, or of the rich!

ONE cannot determine certainly concerning the increaſe or decreaſe of riches merely by the plenty of the circulating coin. We muſt take into the account the paper, and every thing which paſſes currently in commerce. Millions of coin may be exported at particular times, either for war, foreign ſubſidies, or other kinds of foreign ſervice, or to pay for foreign commodities, without the leaſt danger of impoveriſhing the nation. In the laſt caſe, that of purchaſing foreign commodities, we get goods to the value, which, in the courſe of trade, will bring back the money, and will often bring it back *with intereſt*. But it muſt ever be of ſmall conſequence, whether we have the money, or goods which will cauſe the money to return. In the other caſes of war or foreign ſervice, the money, 'tis true, does not return; but it will be only a ſmall part of our money, and a much ſmaller part of our real ſubſtance, that will be exported in

this

this way. And, as it may be neceſſary for our ſafety, ſo a rich commercial nation may be well able to afford this expence, and continue rich and flouriſhing notwithſtanding.

SILVER and gold, which only repreſent more ſubſtantial riches, are of a fluctuating nature. It is not eaſy, it ſeems even impoſſible, to trace their various motions, or determine when they are in greateſt plenty upon the whole. The moſt ſubſtantial riches are more viſible. We may conclude with certainty, that the wealth of any country is increaſed, when the number of the people has increaſed; when the fields and gardens are better cultivated, and produce better kinds, and a greater quantity of fruits; when the country breeds more numerous ſtores, and better kinds of cattle; when the houſes are more magnificent, and more richly furniſhed; when the people are better cloathed, and their tables are more elegant; when their ware-houſes are filled with a more valuable quantity of goods; when the prices of their lands, and moſt other commodities, are raiſed; when their manufactures are increaſed; when their commerce is more widely extended; and there is greater induſtry, than was known in former times. If all theſe ſymptoms, or ſuch of them as are moſt material, concur, the nation muſt certainly

tainly be increasing in riches. In such circumstances the state of the coin is but of small moment. A nation, which, during any particular period, has lost a million of its silver and gold, but improved its lands, and acquired valuable commodities to the extent of ten millions, must be in a better condition at the end of that period, than it was at the beginning of it.

SECT. II.

General Observations concerning the PRE-
SENT OPULENCE *of Great Britain.*

TO apply the obfervations, made in the
laft fection, to Great Britain in particular : One may appeal to the moft incon-
teftable accounts of paft times, and to ocular demonftration at prefent, Whether there
is not a remarkable increafe of valuable improvements, in agriculture and manufactures, fince the Revolution ?

It muft be confeffed, that, during a few
years after the Revolution, before the government was fully eftablifhed, the wars,
which we were obliged to undertake againft
France, lay heavy upon the nation. The
high taxes, which we were obliged to levy
for fupporting thofe wars; the interruption
that was given to trade; the loffes the nation
fuftained both by fea and land; the high intereft and high premiums, that were given
for ready money, before the Government
was reckoned fully fecure; caufed no fmall
diftrefs, perhaps for fome time made the
nation poorer. Undoubtedly they prevented

ed that increase of riches, which otherwise would have been the natural consequence of the security and liberty gained by the Revolution.   Could we have been equally secure, we would have been richer without those wars and taxes.   But it is also true, that, as the Government gained gradually a greater firmness, as the great victories we obtained over the French during the reign of Queen Anne gave great spirits to the nation, as the accession of the family of Hanover to the throne secured the Government and rendered the settlement at the Revolution complete; such a perfect establishment of freedom and security has made trade and riches flow in upon us in a greater proportion than formerly.   This is evident from the augmentation of shipping, the lowness of interest, the increase of rents, and the high price of lands; which the best calculators have determined to be the surest signs of the increase of riches.

THERE cannot be a more unsuspected witness in this matter, than Doctor Davenant, who published several essays upon the trade of England in the end of the last century.   This gentleman cannot be accused of partiality to the Revolution, since he endeavours to shew, that the riches and trade of England were at the greatest heighth in the

year

year 1688, and that both had declined by the expenfive wars and high taxes from the Revolution to the peace of Ryfwick. Yet if we confider the fymptoms he hath marked of flourifhing and declining nations, it will be evident, that, according to his principles, Britain has been greatly enriched fince the peace of Ryfwick *. " A great number " of merchant-fhips, fays he †, efpecially " a great royal fleet that can be readily man- " ned, numerous and coftly buildings, with " rich furniture, great quantities of plate, " rich apparel, great ftores of native ma- " nufactures and foreign commodities, are " the true fymptoms of great wealth." " But——where a nation is impoverifhed by " bad government, by an ill-managed trade, " or by any other circumftance, the inter- " eft of money will be dear, and the pur- " chafe of lands cheap; the price of la- " bour and provifions will be low; rents " will every where fall; lands will lie un- " tilled; and farm-houfes will go to ruin. " The yearly marriages and births will be " leffened, and burials increafed. The " ftock of live cattle muft apparently di- " minifh. Laftly, the inhabitants will by " degrees and in fome meafure withdraw

* In the year 1697.
† In his Difcourfe, " That foreign Trade is bene- " ficial to England."

" them-

" themselves from such a declining coun-
" try." Is this the present condition of
Britain ? If this writer was now alive, would
he not acknowledge, that the state of Britain
is entirely the reverse of what he most prudently foresaw would be the infallible consequence of a bad government, and ill-managed trade ? As the appearances are all of a
contrary nature, he would see with joy, that
Britain has been greatly enriched since he
wrote his discourses.

Mr. Hume, in his Political Discourse of
Interest, considers interest of money as the
true barometer of the State, and its lowness as a sign almost infallible of the flourishing of a people. It proves, says he, the
increase of industry, and its prompt circulation through the whole State, little inferior
to a demonstration.

According to the ingenious Bishop of
Cloyne, the comfortable condition of the
Commons is one of the surest marks of national wealth. Whether, says he, can a
people be called poor, where the common
people are well fed, cloathed, and lodged ?
Again, Whether it be not a good rule where-
by to judge of the trade of any city, and
its usefulness, to observe whether there is a
circulation through the extremities, and whether

ther the people round about are bufy and warm * ?

THESE authorities are of much greater weight, than that of the author of the Three Effays, who is continually crying Poverty. Never, perhaps, was there a more extravagant affertion, than that which we find in the third page, " That, if King William " had conquered France, and given up every " moveable thing in it to indemnify the peo- " ple of England, rich as that country then " was, it would not have been fufficient to " have paid our expences. Nor would " France, after fuch devaftation, have fared " fo ill as England hath done."

IN oppofition to fuch extravagant affertions concerning the poverty of England, it is maintained, in a late Effay upon the National Debt and the National Capital †, That the whole ftock of England, including the coin, the perfonal eftate of each individual, and the whole value of the land, has increafed an hundred millions fterling, during fixty years after the Revolution, more than it had done during fixty years be-

* The Querift, Queries 2d and 532d.
† This Effay was publifhed in 1750, by Andrew Hooke, Efq.

fore

fore it. In the year 1628 it was 333 millions. In the year 1688 it was 616 millions. In the year 1748 it amounted to 1000 millions.

IT is not, perhaps, safe to warrant all the principles and calculations, either of this gentleman, or of any other calculator in political arithmetick. Such calculations can scarce ever be exactly true, tho they are useful to direct our inquiries in these matters. But Mr. Hooke has proceeded on very probable grounds, and sufficiently proved, not only that England is richer, but that it has increased in riches, in a higher proportion since the Revolution, than it had done before *; and that the loud cry of poverty, as the effect of wars and taxes, is wholly chimerical.

WOULD it satisfy those gentlemen, who profess so sincerely to lament the misfortunes of their country, it will be confessed that we have been far from profiting so much, as we might have done, by the Revolution. Considering how chearfully our princes go into every scheme, that is offered to them

* If we are not poorer by the Revolution, we are great gainers upon the whole, as our liberty, and the Protestant religion have been more amply secured.

by

by their parliaments, and what attention is given to the general fenfe of the nation; confidering the princely eftates, and ample powers, and great influence of our nobility and gentry, with the freedom and fecurity of our *Commons*; it might have been expected, we fhould have been both richer and more powerful, than we are. We are neither fo eafy at home, nor fo revered abroad, as our advantages ought to have rendered us. This is owing to the keennefs of our factions, and to a too general want of virtue. But after making juft conceffions on the one fide, it ought to be granted on the other, that, not-withftanding all mifmanagements and weak-neffes, we ftill remain a rich, a great, and a powerful people.

S E C T. III.

Of the Riches of North Britain.

IN a smaller nation, where good agriculture and manufactures have been lately introduced, improvements will be more sensible, than in a kingdom of greater extent, more populous, and where good agriculture and an extensive commerce have been of longer standing. For this reason, tho England is much richer than Scotland, and the improvements of the English much greater, the improvements in Scotland may be more striking and sensible.

In inquiring into the state of Scotland, we shall find so clear an evidence of increasing riches as can scarce be resisted. Nevertheless many in Scotland make loud complaints of poverty, and insist on several phænomena as infallible symptoms of decay. We are able to explain these phænomena, and to shew that they are perfectly consistent with an increasing opulence. Whence we have the strongest presumption, that appearances of the same kind cannot be inconsistent with an increase of riches in England : it will be proper, therefore, to make some observations on the state of Scotland, not only as it is a

part

part of Great Britain, but as they will be useful for illuſtrating the ſtate of England.

THAT the fields and gardens in North Britain are better cultivated, and that the country produces greater ſtores of corn and cattle, can be conteſted by no man in his ſenſes.

THE prices of lands are raiſed from fifteen or ſixteen to at leaſt twenty-three years pur-chaſe. The rents of eſtates and of houſes, and the prices of moſt other things, are alſo greatly increaſed. This can as little be diſ-puted.

As the Scots have more inſtruments and utenſils of all kinds than formerly, ſo they have many more artiſans and manufacturers. They work much more in wood, in iron, copper, and other metals. Nor can any one be ignorant, that their manufactures of cloth are prodigiouſly augmented. Thus both their commodities, and the prices of them, are ſenſibly increaſed; which, accord-ing to an indiſputed maxim, is a ſure ſign of greater wealth.

THEIR ſhipping and commerce is moſt viſibly increaſed. If in ſome few places we ſee fewer ſhips and leſs trade, this is much

more

more than compenſated by the great increaſe of trade in other places upon their coaſts.

IF ſilver and gold were to be accounted the moſt ſolid treaſure, what vaſt additions have they got ſince the Revolution ? Some families perhaps have changed their antique plate for china ware : but what a trifle is this to the additional plate throughout the kingdom ! How few families of any tolerable rank want a decent quantity of plate ? How few had any at the Revolution ?

A ſuperior induſtry is the cauſe of this ſuperior wealth. Before the Revolution there were few manufacturers or artiſans. Agriculture and gardening were in a very low ſtate. The farmers did little more than till and ſow their fields late in the ſpring, and reap them late in autumn. They were idle both in ſummer and in winter. Since that time there is a great addition of artiſans and manufacturers ; and in many places the farmers are employed throughout the whole year. There are ſtill many juſt complaints of idleneſs. The Scots have not equalled the Engliſh in induſtry. But a taſte for improvements in manufactures and agriculture, and an inclination to induſtry, is gaining ground every day in Scotland.

INDUSTRY,

INDUSTRY, indeed, is the great fource of wealth. It avails much more, than filver and gold, or the greateft natural riches. Tho a country be bleffed with a foil capable of producing the fineft crops and of feeding numerous ftores of cattle ; tho there is plenty of natural wood and rich mines ; tho its feas, lakes, and rivers abound with fifhes, and there are fafe and convenient harbours : amidft all thefe natural advantages, it may have few inhabitants, and thefe few may be ill provided for. " Dii omnia vendunt la-" boribus." Without labour a nation may ftarve in the midft of plenty. Without labour every thing muft languifh.

THIS labour is laid out in cultivating the foil, in working in the mines, in fifhing in the feas and rivers, in procuring materials for manufacture at home or abroad, in manufacturing thofe materials, in exporting the overplus, after our own neceffities are fupplied. Thefe materials, either in their natural ftate, or manufactured, become riches to the country. If fpent at home, they make greater numbers live more comfortably ; if carried abroad and exchanged for foreign commodities, bullion or coin, in the courfe of trade, they make an addition to the national ftock. Not only the original prices of all materials, which the country produces,

but

but the price of that labour, which is be-
ftowed on manufacturing and exporting
them ; not only the wages of all the working hands, but the wages of clerks, fuper-
cargoes, and all others who are in any manner neceffary for the merchant, become an
additional fund of wealth, and encreafe the
price to foreigners. The price of labour is
often much greater, than that of the original
materials. Induftry has a thoufand methods,
by which it adds to the wealth of nations.

It is not poffible to eftimate precifely, how
much the Scots have got by their fuperior
induftry. But it is eafy to fee, that they
muft have got a great deal. The labour of
one employed in agriculture may be eftimat-
ed exactly, by knowing the rent of the land,
the neceffary charges of maintaining the la-
bourer, the price of the materials and tools employed in the labour, the price of keeping the
tools in repair, and the price of the produce.
The labour of a farmer's fervant throughout
the year muft maintain the fervant himfelf,
yield him a little at the end of the year, help
to pay the farmer's rent, maintain fuch of
his family as do not labour, and likewife enable the farmer to lay up a little for his children. At this rate, it is very valuable. The
labour of artifans and manufacturers muft be
computed at more, as a greater expence is
neceffary to prepare them for their employment.

ment. But, without pretending to the greateſt exactneſs, let us ſuppoſe every one's labour at a medium to be worth only nine-pence a day, (which can ſcarce be thought too high, ſince many of our artiſans and labourers gain a ſhilling to themſelves, beſides the profit they bring to thoſe that employ them) and computing the number of land-labourers, artiſans, and manufacturers of all kinds, above the number at the Revolution, to be 100,000 *, who work 300 days of the 365, a number which will not perhaps be thought too high, if we conſider how much more labour is employed in agriculture and manufactures, than formerly: by this computation, the value of one year's induſtry will amount to the ſum of 1,125,000 l. above what it was at the Revolution. Whether theſe calculations are perfectly exact or not, whoever conſiders things in this light, will ſee a vaſt ſource of wealth : computing the people of Scotland at a million, if they got ſo great a ſum yearly, it would give twenty-two ſhillings and ſix pence ſterling of additional wealth to every perſon in the kingdom.

* Tho it ſhould be granted, that there were as many hands employed in agriculture before the Revolution, as are at preſent, it is certain there was much leſs labour, ſince many of thoſe hands were idle during a great part of the year.

It

It will be worth while to confider the progrefs of induftry, and to trace out the order, in which it produces its happy effects. This will throw a new light upon the fubject of our inquiry. Notwithftanding the inftability of human affairs, the fame fet of manners may be long preferved, and a country accuftomed to idlenefs and rapine may continue long poor and uncultivated. If a fpirit of induftry is once raifed, and continues to grow, its firft effect is to add to the ftock, and increafe the riches of the country, which, without foreign conquefts, can be done only by increafe of labour. After this, it gradually increafes the number of the people, by furnifhing better means of fubfiftance, and by encouraging marriage. But in fuch a country as Scotland, whither few foreigners refort, it multiplies the people much more flowly, than the riches. The wealth of fuch a nation will be much fooner doubled, than its inhabitants. Nay, a very great increafe of riches, by increafing luxury, may prove a hindrance to marriages, and may prevent a proportionable augmentation of people. Agreeably to fuch principles, it feems evident from ocular infpection, that the riches of Scotland are more increafed than the people. Whence it follows neceffarily, that Scotland is not only richer, but richer in proportion to its inhabitants. From which
another

another conclusion is easily drawn, that, since North Britain has a greater stock of provisions and commodities in proportion to the people, and these commodities do not perish, the Scots must export more, and have a greater foreign trade, than they had in former times.

Thus all the different means of proof concur in establishing his conclusion, That Scotland is much richer than it was at the Revolution, by the increase of agriculture, manufactures, and trade.

SECT.

S E C T. IV.

Objections to what has been asserted concerning the increase of RICHES *in* NORTH BRITAIN *considered.*

NOtwithstanding the arguments for proving that Scotland is much richer, than before the Revolution, such is the force of prejudice, that many in Scotland cannot be convinced of it. They will grant, indeed, what many among the English deny, that *England* has gained greatly by the union of the two kingdoms, but contend earnestly, that *Scotland* has been undone by it. The case is far otherwise. Both England and Scotland have gained greatly : England, by a more perfect peace and security ; so that, having nothing to fear in regard to those parts that lye nearest to Scotland, it can with safety cultivate them to great advantage : Scotland, by a share of the English trade, by a more speedy propagation of the English spirit for agriculture and manufactures, and by the happy progress, that has been made towards a complete rescue of the commons from that slavish dependance which was formerly so common, and still prevails too much, in North Britain.

In

IN truth, the Scots have loſt nothing, that can be called ſubſtantial. They have loſt, indeed, what every nation, which is united to a greater, muſt loſe, even when the union is abſolutely neceſſary for the proſperity of the ſmaller one, and has been eſtabliſhed upon terms greatly to its advantage. The Scots cannot expect to have the *intire* management of affairs upon the north ſide of Tweed. They have loſt the *name* of independance. Two or three of their *old palaces* may poſſibly decay. It would be ludicrous to inſiſt upon the want of the ſplendid proceſſion of their nobility and gentry, and upon the brilliancy of a court, during the ſeſſions of the Scotch parliament. Neither is the greater conſumption, which was occaſioned by thoſe ſeſſions, and which, by the bye, even in thoſe days, was but a trifle to Scotland in general, of much greater importance. To compenſate theſe *trifling* loſſes they have obtained *ſubſtantial* advantages. In place of a *Scotch*, their affairs are under the direction of a *Britiſh* parliament: an aſſembly which is much better conſtituted, has much more authority, and is more able to provide for the general intereſt of Britain, than the Scotch parliament could do for that of Scotland. In place of *empty titles* and an inſignificant pomp, they have acquired the

more

more folid bleffings of fecurity, liberty, and riches.

A great clamour has fometimes been raif-ed about the declining ftate of Edinburgh, the ancient metropolis of the kingdom. No doubt, this city, having formerly been the feat of government, may be fuppofed to have fuffered more in proportion by the Union than moft others ; yet, if we confider the buildings that have been raifed, and the im-provements that have been made in the houfes within the city, the houfes, ftreets, gardens, and other improvements in the neighbourhood, the greater quantity of la-bour and manufactures of various kinds, and the greater ftores of all forts of goods for merchandize ; we will eafily fee upon what infufficient grounds fuch a cry has been raif-ed and fupported.

BUT, if North Britain is become fo much richer, whence is it, it will be faid, that we fee fo many beggars and poor people ? Whence is it, that more merchants become infolvent, and more landed gentlemen fell their eftates, than before the Revolution ? Whence is it, that merchants deal lefs in lend-ing than formerly, and that many farmers are pinched to pay their rents, whofe predecef-fors could lay out money at intereft ? Nay, whence

whence is it, that the number of the people is leſſened, and that we ſee ſo many places in this part of the iſland, that were formerly peopled, now almoſt deſolate, without houſes or inhabitants ? Are not theſe ſymptoms of a declining ſtate ? Neither is it difficult, according to ſuch calculators, to account for this poverty, ſince ſo much money is yearly carried out of the country by the nobility and gentry, who ſpend their eſtates in England; and ſince luxury increaſes ſo faſt, as muſt not only render Scotland ſo poor, but end in a ſpeedy and univerſal ruin. Theſe things are loudly complained of, not only by the diſaffected, but alſo by many ſincere, tho timorous, friends of the Government.

It will be eaſy to account for every one of thoſe phænomena, which is real, notwithſtanding the increaſe of riches; nay, to ſhew, that ſuch appearances may be a natural conſequence of that very increaſe. Speculations of this kind are not diſagreeable, and illuſtrate the nature and effects of induſtry and commerce.

One thing is of the greateſt importance in this argument; nay, the whole reaſoning may be ſaid to depend upon it, " Whether " the number of the people is decreaſing."
When-

Whenever a country is lofing its inhabitants, this is a moft dangerous fymptom. It is true, in a nation confifting of more than a million, we may very well fuppofe, there may be ten thoufand, that are entirely idle and ufelefs. We may fuppofe them incapable either of adding to the riches of a country by their induftry, or of defending it by their counfels or arms. Thefe idle hands may be a burden on the ufeful and induftrious. They may be good for nothing but confuming the produce of the country. Such perfons may be fpared, and the country be better without them. Being freed from the load and expence of maintaining them, the reft of the people will be richer and more able to carry on trade and manufactures. A State can never be richer or ftronger by any but ufeful hands. However, as juftice, humanity, and charity, oblige every nation to maintain many ufelefs perfons ; as it is impoffible to make the diftinction, and export only the ufelefs ; it muft be a bad fymptom in general, when the number of the people is diminifhed.

In a nation where there is a greater ftock of corn, of cattle, and of all forts of commodities, than formerly, if at the fame time the prices of thofe goods, inftead of being diminifhed, are increafed, there muft be more

buyers.

buyers. If it were otherwife, the prices would fall. Again, if there are more buyers, either there muft be more people in the nation for home confumption ; or, if there is not, there muft be a greater export and foreign trade ; upon which fuppofition the nation muft be richer. Which was to be proved.

But, in truth, as the nation muft be richer, we may alfo conclude, that the number of the people will not be diminifhed. A greater foreign trade does not commonly caufe the people to decreafe. Exceffive luxury, the confequence of great riches, may fometimes have this effect ; but luxury has not arrived at this fo fatal heighth in North Britain. It is only when luxury hinders the people from marrying, waftes their health, or renders marriage barren, that it becomes fo baleful. In other refpects, it tends to increafe. If the luxury of great people requires fuch a number of unmarried fervants as puts a ftop to ufeful labour, it muft leffen the number of inhabitants. But, as more work is daily going on in North Britain, and the number of labourers, artifans and manufacturers, is increafing, if the number of idle hands is alfo augmented by the luxury of the Great, the number of thofe in the inferior ranks cannot be diminifhed. Again, as the commons are far from being able to live in luxury, tho

their

their condition is evidently better, their better circumſtances, inſtead of preventing, will rather encourage, marriages ; and, as to thoſe in higher life, tho luxury will have a pernicious effect in other reſpects, yet, their number bearing but a ſmall proportion to that of the whole people, the effects of the luxury of the Great, in diminiſhing the number of the whole people, will ſcarce be obſervable.

Supposing it, therefore, to be certain, from the greater quantity of labour that is carried on, and from the more eaſy circumſtances of the commons, that the number of the people in Scotland is not diminiſhed, it will not be difficult to account for all thoſe appearances, which the Diſcontented inſiſt upon as infallible proofs of a declining condition.

For, 1. tho the people have not been diminiſhed ſince the union of the two kingdoms, yet, in ſeveral places of Scotland, a cuſtom has been introduced of uniting two or three ſmaller farms into one. Several cottagers in particular places have been removed, having been thought idle, and rather a loſs, than an advantage, to the neighbourhood. In other places, ſome arable grounds have been turned into paſturing fields, which require

quire

quire fewer hands to cultivate them. In fome cafes, greater wealth and commerce draw fome from more barren to more cultivated and populous places, from the country to towns, and from the northern to the fouthern parts of Scotland. By thefe alterations, there are fewer people in fome parifhes, than formerly. Yet this deficiency is more than made up by the greater numbers of merchants, fhop keepers, artifans, and manufacturers in towns and greater villages. Thither do the cottagers and land-labourers refort, when they leave their former habitations. Several towns may be named, whofe inhabitants are greatly increafed even fince the rebellion in 1745.

At the fame time, I am far from applauding the fpirit, from which many of thefe alterations may be fuppofed to proceed. It may be laudable at fome times ; it may be no lefs profitable for the Public, than for the landed gentleman, to turn fome fmall farms into one, and fome arable into pafturing grounds. But this humour may eafily go to an extreme : perhaps in fome places it has gone too far already. If thefe changes are made, without any regard to the former poffeffors of thefe farms ; if it is not confidered, by what other means thefe poor families, thus driven from their former habitations,

bitations, can be fupported ; if fuch alterations are not made gradually ; tho they may
be legal, or agreeable to rigid juftice, they
are, in their own nature, barbarous and un-
human, and betray a felfifh and unmerciful
difpofition.

IT may be doubted, whether thefe
cruel landlords truly confult, either their
own, or the public intereft ; at leaft, whether
many improvements of this nature are folid,
and may be expected to be lafting. But be
this as it will, and tho it fhould be found
true, that increafing the extent of many
particular farms yet farther, and throwing
even a greater proportion of our arable into
pafturing fields, would not only enrich the
proprietor, but the Public ; yet as high
prices of grain bear too hard upon the laborious part of the nation ; as turning multitudes of labouring families out of their pof-
feffions, when they have not the means of
fupporting themfelves by labour in fome
other honeft way, muft certainly diminifh
the number of the people ; as in the multitude of the people is the king's honour, and
in the want of them is the deftruction of the
prince *, all meafures, which tend either to

* Proverbs xiv. 28.

cruelty

cruelty or depopulation, ought carefully to be prevented *.

2. In so far as poverty flows from sloth and idleness, it is natural to conceive, that, in a greater number of people, there should be proportionably a greater number of beggars.

3. As the expences of living increase, and luxury prevails, which has truly been the case since the Revolution, and will generally be the case when nations grow richer, the same quantity of money will not go so far as formerly. Consequently, if men gain nothing by industry, but live upon rents, which either are diminished, as has happened to those who live on the interest of money ; or which are not increased, or do not increase, in proportion to the additional expences of living; all such people must become poorer, notwithstanding the general increase of riches. Now there is always a considerable number of persons, who are supported in this manner.

* See Sir Thomas More, the first book of his *Utopia*, and Lord Verulam, in his History of Henry VII. concerning the dangers which may arise from turning arable into pasturing grounds.

4. When

4. When trade is increasing, and a nation is enriched by it, this proves a strong temptation to many to launch out into too extensive schemes, and to venture farther than their stocks will bear. And, as unlucky adventures must often happen, this must necessarily give occasion to more frequent bankruptcies, than will happen in poorer countries where there is little trade. In poor countries there will be but few and small debts; for little credit will be given. In general, therefore, as more people deal in trade, there will be more frequent bankruptcies; and, as the trade is greater, they will be for greater sums. Yet this trade will enrich the country, and these bankruptcies will be of little detriment upon the whole.

5. Tho the increase of industry may greatly augment, and has actually augmented, the value and rents of the lands in Scotland ; yet the lower and middling ranks, the richer merchants, and other gentlemen who do not live upon rents, but by industry, will become sooner easy, and acquire the most early share of the increasing wealth. Such people are generally most frugal, and most attentive to gain. They have neither so keen a taste, nor so much time for expence and luxury, as landed gentlemen, or such as have nothing to do but to pursue their diversions,

verfions. Gentlemen in this condition are commonly moft expenfive at all times. In times of greater riches, they are provoked to greater expence by the general tafte of the nation, and by feeing merchants and others, whom they reckon their inferiors, approaching nearer them in their genteeler method of living. Meanwhile, tho their rents are raifed, they are not raifed fo early as they begin to increafe their expence, or in proportion to their tafte for luxury. Hence, in an opulent commercial nation, a great many of the ancient nobility and gentry will at fome times be obferved to grow poorer, and will at laft be obliged to part with their great eftates to thofe induftrious lawyers, phyficians, merchants, and others, who have been more frugal. We need not, therefore, be furprifed, that, when riches increafe, there are many poor people in a nation. The maxim will hold in general, That, where there are many rich, there will alfo be many poor.

Why, therefore, fhould the writer of the Three Effays * lament fo heavily, that the halcyon days, which were feventy years ago, are miferably changed; and that his friend's eftate of 900 *l.* a year cannot now go fo far,

* Page 33.

as it could have gone in the days of his grand-father? The writer would impute this dif-ference to high taxes; but he ought to im-pute the greateſt part of it to the increaſe of riches. If any gentleman is indolent in not improving his eſtate when he has good op-portunities, what can be expected, but that he ſhould grow poorer, as the nation in-creaſes in riches? This is the natural order of things. It would, ſurely, be too much for the nation, out of complaiſance to an in-active ſquire, to put a ſtop to its induſtry and trade. The eſtate, which in the Three Eſſays is ſaid to be much leſs conſiderable than it was ſeventy years ago, is ſuppoſed to lie in England. The gentlemen of that kingdom, no doubt, deſerve great regard; but a greater regard ſtill is due to the *whole* body of the people. The commons, con-ſiſting of merchants, farmers, and artiſans, are indeed the glory of England. The riches of theſe inferior ranks of men, depending on their freedom and induſtry, according to Mr. Hume *, give the advantage to England above any nation at preſent in the world, or that appears in the records of any ſtory. Scotland has not hitherto had the happineſs to have ſuch wealthy and independent com-mons. However, in its preſent condition,

* In his Political Diſcourſe of Commerce.

it is evident, that the fame fum of money cannot go fo far as formerly, and that thofe, who have made no addition to their eftates, muft appear poorer than in ancient times.

6. WHEN there is much money to be lent by private hands, this is far from being a fure fign of the increafe of riches. To form a certain conclufion, one ought to attend to many different circumftances. If there are many frugal people, who fpend lefs than they have, tho they have but little, what little they can fpare they will be willing to place out at intereft, provided they cannot difpofe of it to better advantage. This muft have been the cafe before the Revolution, fuppofing the fact to be true. But after the union of the two kingdoms, when by commerce with England better methods of agriculture and manufacturing were difcovered, and new fources of trade were opened, as the induftrious part of the nation became richer, inftead of placing out their money at intereft, they often improved their grounds, purchafed a better ftock of cattle, enlarged their manufactures, or extended their trade. This turned to better account, but difabled them from lending. Where there is a great deal of money to be lent, and the lenders are fuch as live on their rents, without induftry or bufinefs; this fhews, that

thefe

thefe perfons live within their income. This is happy for their families, and often profitable for the Public; tho cafes may be put, in which fpending their whole rents, which would prevent lending, may turn out more to the benefit of the country. If, notwithftanding an increafing trade, and an opulent manner of living, the merchant can afford to make purchafes, or place out money at intereft, this is indeed a fign of immenfe wealth. At other times lending money may be a bad fign, and only fhew that the merchant does not know how to turn his money to greater advantage in the way of trade. Thus it is eafy to folve thofe appearances, which are fo frightful to fome unfortunate people, who can never difcern the profperity of their country.

It will be full as eafy to make it appear, that, tho a confiderable fum is yearly carried to England by the nobility and gentry, this does by no means exhauft the country; nor will the argument from this topic anfwer the purpofes of thofe, who raife fo loud a clamour on this head.

It is true, ever fince the union of the two crowns in the perfon of James VI. of Scotland, many of the Scotch nobility and gentry

try

try have been in ufe to fpend fome part of their rents in England. It is alfo true, that more money has been carried to England fince the union of the two kingdoms than formerly. It is confeffed, this is a difadvantage in fome refpects : if 50,000 l. fterling be carried to England yearly, this is much the fame, as if the Scots owed the Englifh the capital of a million, computing the intereft at five per cent. So much are the national riches dimi-nifhed. The Scotch nobility and gentry cannot be vindicated, if, without any real ne-ceffity or juft reafon, they live too much in England, and will not refide at the fine feats of their anceftors even in fummer or autumn. There is certainly a *greatnefs and generofity* in not abandoning our friends or our coun-try when they are poor. Whatever can be juftly conftrued into a contempt of either of them muft be highly criminal. But, after all, great latitude muft be allowed in cafes of this nature. Men are not bound by any tie to live in any particular place, merely to keep money in that fpot of the earth. One need not wonder, that there fhould be fo great a refort to London : fo large and opu-lent a city muft furnifh bufinefs and enter-tainment, to fuit various difpofitions, and to allure multitudes from every quarter. The fame attracting force may be obferved in the

large

large capitals of every other country *. No wonder therefore, that men of rank in Scotland should incline to spend some part of their time in such a metropolis.

WITHOUT inquiring, whether a very large capital is more advantageous, or disadvantageous to a nation; whether the capital of Great Britain is not like a head too large for the body; or, whether Scotchmen are or are not to be blamed for living so much at London; it is evident that North Britain is not impoverished by their resort to the capital; but, on the contrary, is daily increasing in riches; and that the Scots nobility and gentry carry away only a part of their *increased* rents. This, if it were necessary, might be illustrated by a particular computation: but without any calculation, it is ap-

* Aspice agedum hanc frequentiam, cui vix urbis immensæ tecta sufficiunt. Ex municipiis et coloniis suis, ex toto denique orbe terrarum confluxerunt. Alios adducit ambitio, alios necessitas officii publici, alios imposita legatio, alios luxuria, opulentum et opportunum vitiis locum quærens: alios liberalium studiorum cupiditas, alios spectacula: quosdam traxit amicitia, quosdam industria, latam ostendendæ virtuti nacta materiam: quidam venalem formam attulerunt, quidam venalem eloquentiam. Nullum non hominum genus concurrit in urbem, et virtutibus et vitiis magna præmia ponentem.

Senec. in Consolat. ad Helviam, cap. vi.

parent

parent, that the rents in North Britain having been raifed, in fome places to double, in others to a half, a third, or a fourth, more than before the union, and being fcarce diminifhed any where, the addition made to the rents muft be greater than any fum, which the nobility and gentry can be fuppofed to fpend in England. From which it may juftly be concluded, that, fince the union, Scotland has gained in the rents of lands and houfes, as well as in trade and manufactures, and that not a peny of the ancient rent is fpent in England.

The only remaining objection to the affertion, that Scotland is enriched fince the union, is taken from the luxury, that has prevailed fince that period, and is faid ftill to be increafing. But of all objections this is certainly the weakeft. In truth, it proves the contrary to that, which it is brought to eftablifh. Nothing can be more inconfiftent, than, with the author of the Three Effays *, to complain of the fcarcity of gold and filver, of the decay of trade and manufactures, and of the flow progrefs of agriculture, and at the fame time, of the increafe of luxury and expence of living. This writer, indeed, confeffes, that one would fcarcely believe

* Page 19.

fuch

fuch a conjunction could happen. What *may
be believed*, I fhall not pretend to fay : fome
people believe very odly; but, whatever this
writer or any one elfe may believe, one may
venture to affirm, that fuch a conjunction in
any nation is abfolutely impoffible.

GREAT complaints are made of luxury ;
and made moft defervedly. But, in truth,
the increafe of luxury in any nation is an infallible teftimony of the increafe of wealth.
An individual may be worth 5000 l. per
annum, and fpend only a fingle thoufand.
He may augment his eftate without aug-
menting his expences. But this ought never to be fuppofed of a whole people. If a
nation become generally richer, the bulk of
the people will incline to increafe their expences. Landed gentlemen in general are
too much difpofed at all times to go beyond
their incomes, and encumber their eftates.
But, if their rents increafe, their temptations
to live higher will prove ftronger. Even the
induftrious part of the people will add fome-
thing to their former expences, when they
are better able to afford it. If, on the contrary, they do not grow richer, this cannot
be fuppofed of the generality. If luxury is
on the growing hand, riches muft be increafed in proportion. There is only one
exception to this political maxim. For, if

a naa nation is indebted to foreigners for the means of fupporting its luxury ; if foreigners have a juft demand upon it for fums equal to the additional expences above thofe of former times ; it is certainly poorer. What is due to foreigners muft always be fubtracted from the national riches. And, if any nation fpend more than it really has, it muft become poorer, and prove bankrupt at laft. But how little can either South or North Britain be fuppofed to owe to foreign merchants ! I do not fpeak of the public debt ; this fhall be inquired into afterwards : I only confider the debts of private perfons. Now, the balance of what Scotch merchants owe to foreign nations above what foreigners owe to them at any particular time, muft certainly be very fmall, compared with the whole riches of the nation. Nay, the balance may be fuppofed to be often on the fide of Scotland. Other debts, which the Scots owe to one another, are of no confequence in the prefent argument, and do not affect the common riches of the nation.

What abfurd and ridiculous notions are we apt to conceive concerning luxury ! In one fenfe, almoft every thing may be reckoned luxury. In another, there is much lefs than is commonly believed. Defining luxury to be a too elegant or refined, or a too

fump-

fumptuous, method of living, in a moral-
fenfe it is always bad; for it is a great cor-
rupter both of mens genius and virtue. In
a political fenfe, it is alfo bad, as, upon the
whole, it renders a people weak in confequence of their vices. God forbid, that I
fhould endeavour to leffen the horrors, which
wife and good men have moft juftly conceived of it, or that I fhould not prefer the
innocence and virtue of a nation to its riches.
Not only ought a virtuous man to deteft
luxury, but, abftracting from morals, a
found politician, who confiders only the
ftrength of nations, ought to pafs the very
fame judgment. For virtue, by rendering
a people more honeft and valiant, makes
them ftronger either for attack, or for defence; though it does not always render
them opulent. It is only a high degree of
virtue that can fecure good morals and great
riches at the fame time; yet it always tends
to preferve a nation longer, and render it
more fecure. On the other hand, luxury
enervates a people. Yet, where it runs
through all ranks, it can only be fupported
by fuperior riches.

Those maxims, that are juft when applied to the luxury of particular perfons,
cannot always be applied when we confider
a whole people. A private citizen may
fpend

spend more than he has, and may at laſt prove bankrupt. It is altogether improbable, that this ſhould happen to an induſtrious nation. The bulk of an induſtrious people never were, and, according to the common principles of human nature, never will be, diſpoſed to exceed their revenues. Such people are commonly attentive to gain. The love of profit is ſtronger with them, than the love of pleaſure. In conſequence of this they live within bounds, and the far greateſt part of them are frugal. It is chiefly among men of great fortunes, who gain nothing by labour, that we ſhall find the diſpoſition to extravagant expence. In an induſtrious nation theſe form but a ſmall body. Such of them as run in debt, do it gradually. And, as rich induſtrious men come in their places, it is of leſs conſequence to the nation. But we need not put the iſſue of this matter upon probabilities only ; in truth, it is as impoſſible for a whole nation, as for particular perſons, to ſpend more than they have, without being indebted to others. In ſhort, if luxury has been increaſing in Scotland ever ſince the Revolution, riches muſt have increaſed in proportion.

SECT.

SECT. V.

Answers to objections against what has been asserted concerning the wealth of ENGLAND.

IF Scotland is evidently richer than it was before the Revolution, no good reason can be assigned, why England should not be supposed to have been equally fortunate. England is the land of liberty ; London, the center, from which this liberty flows to the rest of the island. The rays of liberty, like those of light, are denser when nearer the center. The Scots are at a greater distance from it. The English are nearer it, and must have peculiar advantages. During several ages, they have been a richer and a more industrious nation. They have had greater skill in agriculture and manufactures, and better notions of trade. In general, they seem to have less curiosity than the Scots, or rather to be more steady in their pursuits. Their artisans and dealers of every kind confine themselves to fewer branches of trade or manufactures, and divert less to other objects not connected with their chief employment. This makes them more expert and successful in those particular branches of trade which they pursue. All these are so great

advan-

advantages, that it is scarce to be thought, the English have not made proportionably greater advances than the Scots; unless it is supposed, that their more early application to trade, and their having carried it to so great a height before the Revolution, hath rendered it impossible, or very difficult, for them to multiply their trade in the same proportion, as may easily be done by the French or Scots, who have more lately applied themselves to commerce.

But, be this as it will, the improvements of England since the Revolution are very great. Compared with England, Scotland is extremely poor; and in all taxes, imposed for the expence of government, ought to be considered in this light. All the signs which indicate an increase of riches are visible in England. Its agriculture is much advanced, the value of land is raised, the interest of money reduced, the quantity of shipping of all kinds, and of the Royal Navy in particular, prodigiously augmented. Numerous stately buildings have been raised, and all things appear grand and magnificent. From all which it might be expected, the minds of the English would be easy upon this point, and not be perpetually haunted with the dreadful spectres of poverty and ruin.

YET

YET not long ago, an essay was published, to prove that the foreign trade of Britain is fast declining. This Essay has been
ascribed to a merchant lately deceased, who
was no less eminent for his riches and extensive trade, than for large and generous
notions of commerce, and for a firm patri-
otism *. A gentleman of such a character
could have nothing at heart but the good
of his country. He could not have any
intention to mislead his countrymen. Yet,
this worthy citizen actually misleads, and
sets before us a very disagreeable view of our
affairs.

NOT only hath he asserted, that the foreign trade of England is declining, but he
seems to infer, that the loss of it makes us
decline in all other respects, and that upon
the whole the nation is growing poor. If
this be not his meaning, or if he would allow, that we are growing rich upon the
whole, we might be less concerned about
our foreign trade, or any particular branch

* Sir Matthew Decker: his book is intituled " An
" essay on the causes of the decline of the foreign
" trade, consequently of the value of the lands, of
" Britain, and on the means to restore both."
This piece seems to have been composed about the
year 1740, and has been printed oftner than once.

of

of that induſtry by which we are enriched.

On this ſubject of foreign trade two ſup-
poſitions may be made. 1. That, tho upon
the whole we are gainers by it, we are
not ſo great gainers as at ſome former period. If this be true, it is a diſadvantage ;
unleſs by applying leſs to foreign trade,
we beſtow our labour at home on an induſtry that is more profitable. It is certainly more profitable to improve our barren lands to the value of a million, than
only to gain half a million by foreign commerce.

2. It may be next ſuppoſed, that, upon
the whole, we are loſers by our foreign
trade ; and our loſs may be computed to a-
mount to a million, or half a million annually,
or to any other ſum. Even upon this ſup-
poſition, we may be growing richer upon
the whole ; for, if we only loſe annually
half a million by our foreign trade, while
we are improving our barren lands and
ſtock of cattle to the value of a million,
we are certainly gaining half a million
yearly.

It may be added, that our gains by domeſtic induſtry, and by the improvement of
our

Our lands and ftock of cattle, are of the moft folid kind. They are more truly profitable than gains to the fame nominal extent by foreign trade. The labours, by which we procure them, are more healthful; they keep our countrymen at home, keep our people more innocent, promote better morals, preferve fimplicity of manners, prevent luxury, and are lefs uncertain and precarious. Foreign trade, no doubt, may be very profitable. In fome cafes, it may bring quicker gains. But our merchants, and many others of our countrymen, value foreign trade too highly, when they lay it down as a pofition, that a nation cannot become rich and powerful without a great and increafing foreign trade.

It is true, if we are every year lofing by our foreign trade, we muft gradually lofe our filver and gold. Not an ounce of either of them will be left among us in the end; and we muft ufe paper or other materials for circulation among ourfelves. According to the author of the Three Effays, and other writers, this is all we have at prefent. Nay, according to the calculations of fome of our merchants, who have been raifing an alarm ever fince the beginning of this century, long before this time there muft not have been a fhilling in the country;

as

as the balance of trade is said to be almost every where against us. But the great quantity of coin and plate that is to be seen, is an infallible proof that there is an error in their computations, and that, upon the whole, the English are still gaining by their foreign trade *.

To give an exact and complete account of the foreign trade of Britain ; to compare the quantity and value of our exports and imports ; to distinguish precisely, when, and where, and how far, the balance of trade is either on our side, or against us ; is too great an attempt for the most skilful of our merchants. It is not proposed to launch out into so wide an ocean. But, without any such detail, it will not be difficult to shew, that Sir Matthew Decker has not proved, that the foreign trade of Britain is declining ; and that all the appearances, upon which he builds his opinion, may be solved upon other principles.

He takes notice † of the long credit taken by shop-keepers ; the great number of

* If the quantity of silver and gold in plate, coin, and bullion, is continually increasing in any nation where there are no mines, that nation must be gaining by foreign trade.

† At the beginning of his Essay.

bank-

bankrupts; the great arrears of rent owing all other England, which the landlords every where complain of; the great number of farms thrown upon the landlords hands ; the vaſt increaſe of the poors rates. All theſe appearances, in ſo far as they are real, have been explained already. They are the natural conſequence of great luxury, and great luxury is the effect of great riches.

BUT, beſide thoſe phænomena already explained, Sir Matthew Decker obſerves, that many petitions are preſented to parliament, complaining of the decay of the woollen manufactures, and of the ſtarving condition to which the poor are reduced in the cloathing countries: two facts, the truth of which I do not examine; for, ſuppoſing them to be true, they prove no more than that one branch of foreign trade is decayed ; which may be ſupplied by others. Trade is very variable in its nature. All the branches of it cannot flouriſh equally at all times. Particular cauſes may make *ſome of them* languiſh at times at which commerce is in the moſt proſperous condition *upon the whole.* When ſeveral nations in Europe, rouſed by the example of the Britiſh, are ſetting up manufactures, and encouraging their people to trade, this muſt neceſſarily produce alterations. No wonder, that our rivals the

French,

French, and other nations upon the continent, seize several branches of commerce; or that our own merchants, intent upon gain, give up a less profitable branch of trade, and prefer a more profitable. As a balance on our side, many branches of trade have been both established, and carried to a great length, since the Revolution; in particular, several, by which we save vast sums, which formerly we paid to the French, and which at present add confiderably to the national wealth *.

The lowness of the price of wool, which is considered as another symptom of the decline of the woollen manufacture and of our foreign trade, may be accounted for, in some measure, by the increase of the breed of sheep in Britain and Ireland, and by the difficulty of smuggling wool into France, notwithstanding the high prices it gives in that country. It is not proposed to examine the state of the wool, or how far the woollen manufacture is decayed. This is a subject more proper for others, than for the author of the Characteristics. But it may be observed in general, that the cheapness of the materials is an advantage to a manu-

* See Poftlethwayt's Univerfal Dictionary of Trade and Commerce, under the article TAXES.

facture;

facture; and that materials may increase so much, that their prices may be low even when there is a great demand for the manufacture into which they are wrought.

THE other bad symptoms of a declining foreign trade, that are mentioned by this writer, arise from the state of the exchange, bullion, and coin. It is said, the exchange was more against us in the year 1740, than formerly. But does any man know, how the exchange stands between London, and *all* the places with which the English trade? or does he know, how much we lose or gain by every city, or by every branch of trade? Except he know this in the constant course of trade, he cannot know how the exchange stands upon the whole, or draw firm conclusions from the course of it.

THE scarcity of silver coin is given as another sign of the declension of our foreign trade. But if we have greater plenty of guineas and of foreign gold, this will compensate the scarcity of silver. There is an obvious reason for this scarcity: our silver and gold coins are not properly adjusted in proportion to the rest of the coins in Europe; so profit may be made by exporting the latest coined and the heaviest of our silver money. This is a loss, no doubt;

but

but it doth not prove, that our foreign trade declines.

THE laſt bad ſymptom, obſerved by the writer of the Eſſay, is that the mint lies idle, and that little or no new coin appears. On this, he lays down two maxims, both of them fallacious. " The barometer of the " general trade of a nation is its mint. If " plenty of treaſure is brought in, and " little carried out, part of it will be con- " tinually coining, and much new money " will appear; the certain ſymptom of a " flouriſhing trade *." Is not the reverſe rather to be expected? and may not the maxim be turned another way? " If plenty " of money is brought in, and little carried " out, the coin will not be diminiſhed, but " be increaſed. There will be no neceſſity " for a new coinage; ſo little new money " will appear: the certain ſymptom of a " flouriſhing trade."

THIS argument will appear ſtronger, if we conſider the circulation of paper.

HIS ſecond maxim is of the ſame kind. " + If much treaſure be brought in, yet " more be carried out, the mint muſt lie

<hr>

* Eſſay, page 3.　　　　　　† Ibid.

" idle

" idle. Little new money will appear ; the
" fure fign of a decaying trade." The reverfe appears rather to be the truth : " If
" much money be brought in, yet more be
" carried out, the mint muft not lie idle,
" as coin will be daily more fcarce. There-
" fore there will be a great deal of new
" money appearing ; the fure fign of a de-
" caying trade." However, as merchants
are beft able to judge of thefe maxims, it
is beft not to be pofitive on this fubject of
the mint: only, in general, it feems to be
true, that a greater or lefs quantity of coin
is not a *certain* fign, either of increafing poverty, or of growing riches.

Thus, notwithftanding his knowledge of
trade, this eminent merchant has not proved,
that the foreign trade of England hath declined. Such a decline is not probable,
fince the number of merchants and of fhips
is daily increafing. It is fcarce to be thought,
that our merchants would perfift in carrying
on a lofing trade. We fee the very fame
appearances as if we were gaining : for, if
our merchants are gaining, whatever they
gain muft, at laft, be brought to our fields,
cities, and harbours Merchants can fecure their gain no where elfe, except they
lend it to foreigners, or place it in foreign
banks. I do not find, this is alleged.
Wealth

Wealth is thought to be no where so safe as in Britain. We see daily additions made to our shipping. Our harbours are in a better condition. There is plenty of naval stores. We have all sorts of foreign commodities. Our own fields are better cultivated. Therefore the presumption certainly is, that our foreign trade, as well as our domestic industry, is increased. But, after all, the question of the greatest importance is not, " Whether we gain or lose by foreign trade ?" The more important inquiry is, " Whether " we are growing richer or poorer upon the " whole ? ' If it would put an end to disputes about foreign trade, more might be granted, than can possibly be demanded by such as are most anxious about it. Grant that during the last sixty years we have lost half a million yearly by foreign trade, or, which is the same thing, have exported bullion or coin to that value, amounting in the whole to thirty millions ; the most timorous dealers in exchange can ask no more. So great a loss seems absolutely impossible, considering the immense quantity of additional plate that has been got within this period. Yet, even upon this hard supposition, as the nation has gained to a much greater value by the improvement of our lands and home manufactures, we are a great deal richer upon the whole.

WE

WE ought not, however, to neglect the good advice of this worthy citizen. He has faid enough to put us upon our guard, and hath fuggefted many ufeful methods for recovering fome branches of trade, which we may have loft, and for improving fuch as may be in danger. The nation is, undoubtedly, greatly obliged to him for his good wifhes and ufeful endeavours ; but he has been mifled by the greatnefs of the commerce of England. The Englifh have been continually improving their trade from the days of Queen Elizabeth : fo it is at length come to a great height. The advantages, which they have gained by it, have ftirred up the emulation of other nations. Ever fince the reign of Lewis XIV. the French have made great efforts to rival us in trade. Being an ingenious and ambitious nation, they have fucceeded very far in their defign. Viewing the great advances which the French have made, and which are more fenfible during the laft forty years, one is apt to imagine, that the Englifh trade, though really much greater, begins to decline. As it was great before, the later increafe of it becomes lefs perceptible. It is impoffible, in the nature of the thing, that the trade of any nation can be *continually* increafing, and bring in greater and greater fums in a perpetual fucceffion. It muft often be at a ftand.

ftand. It may often be fo great, that it will not be eafy to enlarge it. It may often appear to decline, when it is really, though infenfibly, increafed. But, while we fee fuch goodly appearances and improvements in our fields, cities, and harbours, we have infallible teftimonies of increafing riches.

It is not however intended to affert, that our country might not be much more improved, and the commerce of Great Britain rendered much more flourifhing. It would be eafy to propofe many excellent fchemes for promoting this defign. Many notable ones have been offered to the Public with this view. Among others, Sir Matthew Decker, and Mr. Tucker of Briftol *, have made fome grand and magnificent propofals for raifing taxes more advantageoufly for the Public, and for improving and embellifhing our country. Such propofals merit the higheft applaufe ; they difcover an exalted patriotifm, and an enlarged mind, and juftly deferve the notice of men in power. Could *any* thing tend fo much to their honour, as giving due attention to public-fpirited fchemes, felecting fuch of them as are juft and practicable, and employing

* In his excellent Effay on the advantages and difadvantages which refpectively attend France and Great Britain, with regard to trade, &c.

their

their intereſt and authority to have them eſtabliſhed ? How hard is it, that ſo many are wholly taken up with their own ſelfiſh and *little* views, in procuring a precarious power, when they might obtain a more honourable and ſolid intereſt, by *real ſervices* to the Public! When it is ſo eaſy to ſhew the advantages of many noble propoſals, it is unhappy, that it ſhould be found ſo difficult to put any one of them in execution.

But while Sir Matthew Decker deſerves the higheſt praiſes for endeavouring to correct our errors, he has fallen into a miſtake concerning the effects of our taxes at preſent. For the ſame reaſons, for which we have taken notice of other errors in his Eſſay, it will be neceſſary to correct his miſtake on this head ; as it has raiſed too great an alarm, and tends too much to diſquiet the minds of the people.

According to this gentleman's principles *, when the Government raiſes 4,650,000 l. by exciſes, cuſtoms, and ſalt duties, and raiſes ten per cent. or 465,000 l. for collecting them, both ſums amounting to 5,115,000 l. the people pay in conſequence no leſs than 10,869,375 l. and add-

* Page 35.

ing

ing the poor's rate, and the reft of the taxes, which he calculates at 4,420,000 l. the fum of all the taxes amounting at this rate to 15,289,375 l. he concludes, that, computing the people of England at eight millions, and their expences at 8 l. per head, (64 millions in the whole) more than 31 per cent. of their whole expences is chargeable on the taxes.

This is a high calculation. The method of inftituting it is fomewhat intricate. It is fuppofed that thofe, who pay the five millions immediately to the Government, muft, on this account, raife the prices of their goods to their cuftomers. Thefe cuftomers, again, muft lay the advanced prices of the goods, which they have bought, on the cuftomers to whom they fell them. Thefe, again, muft lay the advanced prices upon their cuftomers; and fo on in fuccesfion, through all the orders and individuals in the State, till, at laft, the goods arrive at the confumers.

Without infifting, that this argument, if it is folid, muft affect trade in *all* countries, where taxes are levied by cuftoms or excifes, and fo muft affect *our rivals* as well as ourfelves; it is, in its own nature, too fubtile; it is built on too precarious principles,

ciples, to be convincing, and feems more fuitable to a *metaphyfician* than a merchant. This will be evident from a few obfervations.

ACCORDING to Sir Matthew Decker, fince the price of fhoes muft be advanced by the tax on leather, the grazier, the butcher, the tanner, the leather-cutter, and the fhoemaker, who buy each from the other in fucceffion, muft lay upon their cuftomers, firft, the advanced prices of the fhoes they wear; fecondly, the advanced prices of the wages of their journeymen, who muft raife their wages to anfwer the advanced prices of fhoes; thirdly, the money paid on account of all the former advanced prices, in confequence of the tax; and laft of all, a reafonable profit on this money as traders. At this rate this writer mufters up twelve advanced prices in fucceffion, which the wearers of fhoes muft pay for the tax, beyond the bare duty. And as both foap and candles are taxed, he places twelve advanced prices more on fhoes, on account of the tax on foap, and other twelve on account of that on candles. He obferves further, that the fame thing muft hold in all taxes on the neceffaries of life; and that the dearnefs of all neceffaries muft advance the price of all labour, and force the mafter-tradefmen to

raife

raife on their cuftomers the taxes and advances on their confumption.

By thefe methods he finds, that the fubjects, who confume the goods, pay more than the double of the tax which is levied by the Government.

But all thefe calculations feem to be founded on conjecture alone. And their uncertainty will appear, if we confider, that any reafonable rule, which can be laid down for eftimating thefe advanced prices, muft carry the matter much farther than Sir Matthew Decker himfelf hath computed, or than any man can admit.

The moft equitable rules for making any probable computation feem to be (1.) That every perfon whatfoever, who fells his goods, or labour, in the way of trade, from the firft who pays the tax immediately to the Government, to the laft who furnifhes the goods to the confumers, muft exact from his cuftomers not only all the money which he paid on account of the tax but a reafonable profit on this money, in the way of trade, as well as upon that part of his ftock which is laid out on the prime coft of goods. (2.) That as the common intereft on money is reckoned too fmall a profit in trade, a
greater

greater profit muft be allowed on the money that is paid on account of the tax. At which rate, thefe profits may be computed at 10, at 15, or at 20 per cent. and in fome cafes will reach higher.

THIS cafe will be fimilar to that of compound intereft; in which, if the intereft is at 5 per cent. the principal is doubled in fewer than 15, tripled in fewer than 23, and quadruplicated in fewer than 29 years. If the intereft is fuppofed to be 10 per cent. the principal is doubled in fewer than 8, tripled in fewer than 12, and quadruplicated in fewer than 15 years. If the intereft is fuppofed to be 20 per cent. the principal is doubled in fewer than 4, tripled in fewer than 7, and quadruplicated in fewer than 8 years. Computations of the fame nature may be made for other higher proportions.

Now as Sir Matthew computes no fewer than twelve advanced prices on fome taxes, and, according to his method of calculating, might undoubtedly, in feveral cafes. reckon more; and as the profits of merchants on money laid out in trade may be fuppofed always more than 5, and fometimes more than 10, 15, or even 20 per cent. it is eafy to fee, that taxes ought to be raifed to the confumers,

fumers, not only to double, but to triple, quadruple, nay, in a higher proportion; which yet no man can poffibly imagine to be true. There muft be a fallacy therefore in this argument. Little ftrefs can be laid on fuch computations. So the people of Britain need not be greatly alarmed at the taxes impofed by cuftoms and excifes. And if there is no fallacy, they are in no worfe condition than other nations.

I do not however enter minutely into the nature of fuch taxes; and fhall not affert, that the Government might not raife equal fums, with greater eafe to the people. I approve of many of the fchemes fuggefted by Sir Matthew Decker and others, and wifh that a fpirit of patriotifm may prevail more and more, to render them effectual.

PART

PART IV.

Of the Payment of the National Debts.

IF Britain be confidered at prefent with refpect to piety, morals, or publick fpirit ; if we examine the national genius, either for the nobler arts and fciences, or for war ; no doubt, there are many things alarming in our condition. But nothing, that relates *only to money*, or *to trade*, ought to give anxiety to true patriots, excepting perhaps the greatnefs of the public debts. For tho we have fufficient funds for fupporting the public credit, and for clearing the national debts, yet great debts are *embarraffing* in their own nature, and unlefs they are prudently managed, may, in certain circumftances, involve us in difficulties and confufion. For this reafon every lover of his
country

country fhould ardently wifh to have the public debts paid, and fhould chearfully contribute his endeavours towards fo good an end.

AT the fame time, there is no juft reafon to apprehend, that the nation either is impoverifhed by thefe debts in the mean time, or is unable to clear them without diftrefs, whenever they fet heartily about it. There is a fund of wealth in Great Britain, I do not fay inexhauftible, but fuperior to that of any other European nation, not excepting even the Dutch, who, notwithftanding their immenfe trade and vaft quantity of filver and gold, are far from having fuch folid funds, or being in fuch advantageous circumftances, as the Britifh. Great Britain has fubftantial funds vaftly fuperior to all our debts and neceffities, even tho we are engaged in war.

SUPPOSING that we owe eighty millions ; eighty millions do not exceed, or only exceed a very little, perhaps they do not even amount to, the yearly revenues of the people of Great Britain and Ireland. According to Davenant's calculation for the year 1688, there were more than five millions and a half of people in England, each of whom, at a medium, fpent 7 l. 9 s. 3 d.
a year.

a year. Whether we confider the number of the people, or their yearly expence, the computation was not too high. It is computed, there are ten millions of people in Great Britain and Ireland at prefent. And, as there are fuch high complaints of our luxury, we may allow 8 l. 10 s. for every man's expence, or eighty five millions for the expences of the whole people. Again, fuppofing that a fourth part, or twenty of the eighty millions, are due to foreigners, and that we export a million annually to pay the intereft at five per cent. at this rate, the yearly revenues of the people of Great Britain and Ireland, after paying what they owe to foreigners, do not amount to lefs than eighty-four millions fterling*. With fuch a vaft fund of wealth, can we be at a lofs to fall upon proper methods of difcharging the whole, or what part of the public debts we find neceffary ? Were we to confider the whole nation, as a private gentleman of a

* The author of the Three Effays has not a juft conception of the wealth of England when he imagines (page 11.) that the Englifh could not hold it long without being undone, if they were obliged to fend 600000l. yearly out of the country. They ought not, for no nation ought, to give away their money without good reafons ; but tho they fent away a greater fum, they would not be foon exhaufted.

good

good eſtate, who owed no more than a year's rent, it would give us a favourable proſpect of our affairs. There is certainly ſome ſort of reſemblance. Tho the iſland, or the rents, trade, and induſtry of the inhabitants, cannot be ſold like an eſtate; yet the public revenues, or the revenues of the whole people are like a perpetual annuity; and if a nation in ſuch circumſtances would raiſe their taxes, and ſpend no more than formerly, like a private gentleman, who raiſes his rents without increaſing his expences, they muſt be able to pay their debts, without being in the leaſt incumbered.

But leaving it to his majeſty and the parliament to conſider, how ſuch ſalutary ſchemes may be beſt effectuated, methinks it would not be difficult for private perſons, with no very great degree of public ſpirit, to aſſiſt greatly in accompliſhing this excellent deſign, nay, to accompliſh it without any loſs to themſelves, and without any augmentation, nay, with an abatement of the taxes. There is no myſtery in all this. If the ſtory be true, the honeſt man, who lately ſent 100l. to one of the miniſters of ſtate to help to pay the public debt, has led the way and ſet us a fair example. Nay he has done more than is neceſſary. For there is no neceſſity for private perſons to advance their money.

money. It would be sufficient, if the richer fort would voluntarily entruft the Government with their plate, and fubmit to the fmall inconveniency of wanting the ufe of it for a feafon. In imitation of the generofity of fuch a worthy citizen, who contributed an hundred pounds for fo good an end, may a public fpirit fpread itfelf among the people, and every one run with his plate to the public treafury, that the public debts may be more fpeedily paid! What an immenfe quantity of plate is there in this ifland! How many millions of the national debt might be fwept off by it at once! This would be an advantage to the Government, if no intereft were demanded for the ufe of the plate. The benefactors of the Public would fuffer no lofs, fince their plate is a dead ftock to them at prefent, and they would have parliamentary fecurity for its being repayed with the full value of the tax upon the plate and of the original workmanfhip. Mean time, let thofe taxes, which are underftood to be the moft burdenfome, or to bear hardeft on our trade, be abolifhed, and only fuch as are eafily borne be continued for fome years longer. In this method, in the firft place, what is at prefent the national debt, and bears intereft, or what part of it fhould be thought proper ; and next the new debt, might be cleared. Can parting with our

plate

plate in this manner be said to require a very *high* strain of public spirit ? How easily may plate be wanted ! How honourable to want it on such an occasion ! Might not a few grand examples render the want of it fashionable ? Might not the whole nation be engaged in such a scheme with eagerness, and every man, who had plate, rejoice in having an opportunity of contributing to the good of his country ?

WE have not the least reason to apprehend, that there is any *necessity* for such a scheme, nor to dread any danger to the public credit. The British legislature is sufficiently able, and, we trust, will not fail, to take care of the public welfare. But it becomes subjects under such a happy constitution to attempt what is great and generous, and to shew a forwardness to secure their free government against the most remote dangers. The slaves of an absolute monarchy need give themselves no trouble about their government, they cannot be *worse* than they are ; but the subjects of Britain are blessed with a constitution, worthy to be preserved till the end of time.

ANY scheme of offering our plate to the Public may, indeed, be thought romantic. It is so, perhaps ; and can hardly be expected ed to fucceed in an age nowife remarkable for public fpirit. But it is generous at leaft. If we are difpofed to go beyond the common rate, it is better to imitate thofe heroes of romance, who were remarkable for juftice and magnanimity, than, as if we were *heroes* of a *different* character, and *indifferent about honefty*, imitate the author of the Three Effays in fuggefting inglorious fchemes of ftopping the credit of public banks, and in endeavouring to excite opulent nations to defraud their creditors by abolifhing the public debts, inftead of honeftly paying them. Let the minifters of a defpotic monarchy applaud fuch fraudulent counfels. Let tyrants break their faith, and abufe the people, whom under the pretence of loans they have forced to furrender their money : but let the citizens of fo opulent a nation as Britain, let the happy fubjects of fuch a free government, be afhamed of difhonourable propofals, and deteft infinuations of violating public engagements. Such counfels are equally contrary to the commercial interefts of Great Britain, and to the fpirit and genius of the Britifh conftitution. The Britifh government would not fuffer fuch propofals to be openly made without teftifying their indignation at them, did they not confider their honour and faith as above all fufpicion,

and

and treat even the moſt peeviſh and diſcontented children with a more magnanimous
indulgence, than an abſolute monarch dares
venture to allow to the greateſt favourites
among his ſlaves.

PART

PART V.

Of the National Genius and Capacity for Self-Defence.

WHILE the people of Britain are possessed of great wealth, and enjoy the most ample liberty, a British author has lately started up *, who,

* The author of The Estimate of the Manners and Principles of the Times.

Tho this book has gone through several editions in a short time, it cannot be, from thence, inferred, either that the taste of the age is not so superficial, as the author has asserted, or that his book is unluckily adapted to this superficial taste. A solid and useful book may sometimes have a run in a superficial age; and *vice versa*. However, it is easy to account for the popularity of such pieces as the Estimate. The writer of it had no reason to imagine, that his design was not popular. Few things are more popular, than severity against national vices. Those divines, who paint their audience blackest, raise the most dreadful spectres, and speak the worst of the times and of human nature, frequently are the most popular. One may often observe whole

granting

granting all, that can be demanded on either of thefe heads, maintains at the fame time, that Britain is going faft to deftruction. According to this author, our liberty has degenerated into licentioufnefs, and our wealth has produced fuch an effeminacy of manners, as has almoft extinguifhed the good principles, and deftroyed the genius and capacity, of the nation. If it can be reckoned any happinefs, he indeed allows, that there is fcarce fo much courage remaining, as will excite us to a civil war, or raife violent commotions at home. He is not therefore apprehenfive of any internal danger *. But he pronounces us fo defencelefs againft foreign nations, that we run the greateft rifk of becoming an eafy prey to any bold invader, and in particular of falling before the fuperior genius of the French.

Tho both charity and juftice forbid us to impute any bad defign to this author, it is not eafy to find out the good tendency of his performance. It may be kind, no doubt, to hold up a true mirror to the Public †, and to fet the vices of the age in a proper light: but whatever benefit may be expected from a

companies more highly entertained with frightful tales, and h rrible relations, than with the moft juft defcriptions of nature and of human life.

* Eftimate, p. 125.　　　† Eftimate, p. 15.

true

true mirror or a juſt repreſentation of errors and misfortunes, it is dangerous to preſent a glaſs of ſuch an unlucky conſtruction, as diminiſhes moſt of the beauties, and magnifies blemiſhes ſo much, that he who ſees his face in it is in hazard of being frighted out of his ſenſes, of ſwooning away at the ghaſtly appearance.

WHAT the author of the Eſtimate imagines to be a mirror, ſeems rather to be an inſtrument of this unfortunate kind. This gentleman has unluckily fallen into the ſame error, for which he blames the " ſpe-
" culative and virtuous in every age, who
" have been apt to aggravate its manners
" into the higheſt degree of guilt. to ſati-
" rize rather than deſcribe, and to throw
" their reſpective times into one dark ſhade
" of horror *."

I ſincerely lament the impiety of the age. I am ſorry there ſhould be ſuch good reaſon to complain of our bad morals, and of our want of public ſpirit. I am far from approving many of our methods of education. I much diſlike the reigning taſte and diverſions of many of our men of faſhion and politeneſs. I moſt heartily condemn their paſſion for gaming, their luxury, effeminacy, and falſe delicacy. I would not affirm, that

* Eſtimate, p. 27.

the

the national genius and capacity for fcience, legiflation, or war, is the higheft of the kind, or that we have philofophers or poets equal to fome in former times. We cannot pretend to have generals equal to the duke of Marlborough, or fuch feamen as admiral Blake. In fhort, our vices and weakneffes are too evident not to be confeffed, and moft fincerely lamented by every good man. Yet we are not fo deftitute of genius and capacity, as is maintained by the author of the Eftimate. If he intends to fay, as feems very probable *, that his country has loft its fame, and that his countrymen in general are become the contempt of Europe, he hath certainly carried the matter too far. The Britifh are by no means contemptible; for with all their weakneffes they are envied and admired among the neighbouring nations.

If we confider in what age or nation, upon a due comparifon of all circumftances, one would have chofen to live, it may be affirmed with lefs caution, than is ufed by the author of the Eftimate, " That there is " no time nor country, delivered down to us " in ftory, in which a wife man would wifh " fo much to have lived, as in our own †,

* Eftimate, page 83, 84.

† The author of the Eftimate, page 15, puts it no higher, than that a wife man would wifh this " in

for

for there is no time nor country, delivered down to us in ftory, in which the body of the people have lived in fuch plenty, liberty, and fecurity.

IF we confider our principles and manners, as indications either of our virtue or depravity, or of our genius or want of capacity, this author's affertions, after all his foftenings and limitations, are unreafonably fevere. In no other light can we view feveral expreffions, " That religion is evidently *deftroyed* in " England †; That the honeft pride of vir- " tue is *no more* ‡ ; That the principle of " honour is either loft or totally corrupted ; " That no generous thirft of praife is left " among us § ; That the principle of pub- " lic fpirit or love of our country is perhaps " lefs felt among us, than even thofe of re- " ligion and true honour ‖." The author has indeed exprefsly declared, that there are exceptions : but upon the whole he is too fevere.

IF we confine the inquiry into our principles and manners according to the plan of

" fome refpeéts." But he might have put it much ftronger.

† Eftimate, page 175. ‡ Ibid. page 59. § Ibid. page 61. ‖ Ibid. page 62.

this

this writer, and the leading queſtion ſhall be, " How far the preſent ruling man- " ners and principles of this nation may tend " to its continuance or deſtruction * ?" this author has much miſtaken our circumſtan- ces, and pronounces too boldly on our weak- neſs and want of defence.

" THAT fortune by no means rules the " world; that there are general cauſes, na- " tural or moral, which operate in every " State, and which raiſe, ſupport, or over- " turn it †, " will be diſputed by none. Nevertheleſs, every defeat, or unſucceſsful expedition, is not to be aſcribed to the man- ners and principles either of the whole peo- ple, or of thoſe of higher rank ; but may often be accounted for by particular cauſes.

THE greateſt, wiſeſt, moſt proſperous, virtuous, and magnanimous nations, in times of their greateſt proſperity and virtue, have met with greater diſappointments and defeats, than the Britiſh have met with in the preſent war. Four times were the Ro- man armies beaten by Hannibal in Italy it- ſelf in the beginning of the ſecond Punic war. Our misfortunes have not been ſo great, nor of ſuch long continuance, that

* Eſtimate, page 24.　　‡ Ibid. page 12, 13.

we

we muft impute them to a general ftupidity or cowardice, either of thofe in lower or higher ranks. Other reafons undoubtedly may be affigned for them.

It is dangerous to decide haftily in fuch cafes. Whether particular victories or defeats are owing to fome particular caufe, or ought to be underftood as the effects of the general temper and genius of a nation, is often a perplexed queftion: it is often impoffible to be determined, except by thofe who know the fecret fprings of action. It is often an ufelefs queftion, and frequently iffues in a difpute rather about words than things. Without detracting from the wifdom of the Britifh councils, or from the bravery of the Britifh troops, during the war in the reign of queen Anne, there are, at leaft, plaufible reafons for afcribing no fmall part of our fucceffes in that war to the incomparable military genius of the duke of Marlborough. At fome particular times the fafety and glory of a nation has been known to depend upon a fingle man, or upon a very few. In great nations this will rarely happen, if they are not fubjected to a defpotic monarch. When it happens, the fituation is very dangerous. But fuch is not the cafe of Britain at prefent. We ftand on a broader bottom, and our national

tional capacity for self-defence rests upon a surer foundation.

By the concessions of the author of the Estimate, " the character of the manners of
" this age and nation is by no means that
" of abandoned wickedness and profligacy *.
" The common people of this nation seem
" possessed of bodily strength, hardiness, and
" courage. There are no better fighting
" men upon earth. They seldom turn their
" backs upon their enemy, unless when their
" officers shew the way, and even then are
" easily rallied, and return to the charge
" with the same courage †. The spirit of
" liberty happily still subsists among us,
" tho not in its genuine vigour. The love
" of liberty is not extinguished. We all
" wish to continue free ; nay, in his opinion,
" the spirit of liberty hath been ingrafted
" by the arts of policy in other countries,
" but shoots up here, as from its natural
" climate, stock, and soil : whence its de-
" struction by external violence will pro-
" bably be no more than temporary ‡. The

---

* Estimate, p. 26.　　† Ibid. page 88, 89.
‡ Estimate, p. 17—20.
This is the most comfortable prospect the author of
the Estimate hath given us of the affairs of Britain.
Despotism prevails almost universally. Mankind are
enslaved by tyrants. An arbitrary power rages in the
" writer

writer likewife allows us " humanity, or
" pity to the diftreffed ;" and perhaps flatters

world. Among the few nations, which have preferved
their liberty, Britain fhines foremoft in riches and fame.
But according to the author of the Eftimate we are
rolling to the brink of a precipice; Britain finks under
the fuperior genius of the French ; the fatal hour approaches, and its liberty is in great danger of being
deftroyed by external violence. Slender are the hopes
he gives us of efcaping : the probability lies againft us:
our deliverance is only poffible. " A defpairing nation,
" (fays he, page 221) *may yet* be faved, by the wif-
" dom, the integrity, and unfhaken courage of fome
" great minifter." I dare fay it is true : but if Britain
is as much funk in indolence, cowardice, and venality,
as this writer apprehends, it is fcarce poffible. Even
the great king William, who will be acknowledged to
have been as able a ftatefman as any who can afpire to
be a minifter at prefent, notwithftanding the wifdom
and rectitude of his fchemes, is fuppofed to have been
obliged, contrary (as will be confeffed) to his natural
difpofition, to oppofe the national turn, by filencing
all he could with places or penfions. The power of a
minifter at prefent, (in times confeffed to be more corrupted) can fcarce be fuppofed greater but in fo far as
he has it in his power to filence a greater number by
the fame methods. This only cherifhes the difeafe,
brings us nearer to the crifis, and renders our deftruction more certain. Our ruin therefore, according to
this writer, may be called next to inevitable. But he
gives us greater hopes of recovering our liberty, and,
of confequence, our former glory and felicity, tho
liberty fhould be deftroyed by external violence. " It
" is probable (fays he) its deftruction will be no more
" than temporary." In this ifland " liberty fhoots up
" as from its natural climate, ftock, and foil." To
the prefent generation this may be thought to give little

us

us too much, when he adds, " That huma-
" nity is natural to the nation, and that the
" nation hath always been diftinguifhed by
" ir, and poffeffes it in a higher degree than
" other countries *." He likewife allows
us another virtue, which he grants to be of
the higheft confequence, " the pure admi-
" niftration of juftice, as it regards private
" property †." Thefe are goodly materials, not only for preferving internal peace
and happinefs, but for defending us againft
external force. The ftrength and good
principles of the common people in any
country, efpecially in Britain, where they
are more high fpirited than any where elfe,
ought not to be reckoned fo defpicable as
the writer of the Eftimate imagines ‡. We

comfort: to the cowardly, effeminate, and felfifh it
will give none: but how confolatory is it to the generous and difinterefted lovers of Britain, who can be
happy in forefeeing the grandeur and felicity of their
country in fucceeding ages! To fome fuch extenfive
profpect, or to a fublime philofophical idea of this kind,
" the prefent deftruction, even of the greateft nation,
" is of fmall confequence in the univerfe," it muft have
been owing, that the writer of the Eftimate, amidft his
melancholy profpects of the prefent ftate of Britain,
fhould appear fo calm and compofed, as to be able to
ftudy elegance of phrafe, and fearch after thofe antitl e-
fes and elaborate turns of expreffion, which occur every
where in this book.

* Eftimate, page 21, 20.   † Ibid. page 22.
‡ Eftimate, page. 25.

may

may reasonably expect, that their force and weight would not be insignificant against a foreign invasion, tho deliverance should not arise from any other quarter; and that in times of extremity (according to the language of the Estimate) some leading mind or superior intelligence would naturally arise from among themselves to give impulse and direction to their enterprizes in defence of their country †. If the love of liberty about a century ago roused them to defend their rights against a powerful party at home, and inspired them with matchless valour, may it not be expected, that the posterity of those men, the robust and hardy commons of the same nation, not enervated by the luxury of the Great, but inured to labour, would, in a time of extremity, be stirred up to defend their country, and all that was dear to them, against any army that could possibly invade them from France.

BESIDES the natural strength and courage of our commons, and the acknowledged remainder of a spirit of liberty, humanity, and regard to property, diffused through all ranks; if we compare ourselves with our neighbours on the continent, in particular with our rivals the French, whose maxims

† Estimate, p. 25.

and

and policy are fo greatly extolled in the Eftimate *, we have no reafon to grant, that we
are deftitute of the means of felf-defence in
the genius and principles of thofe of higher
rank.

WHAT caufe have the Britifh nobility and
gentry given their countryman to imagine,
they have lefs military honour and public
fpirit than the French? A few individuals
may behave ill. Both French and Britifh
officers have turned their backs; the French
as often, and as difhonourably, as the Britifh. But what is this to either of the nations? or muft our officers in general be
therefore reckoned ftupid or cowardly? Either of the nations may produce greater men
in every profeffion at fome particular times
than at others. But from nothing, that has
happened of late, have we juft ground to
eftablifh an uniform preference in favour of
the French. A Britifh army at prefent will
not be afraid to meet the French in any
field with equal numbers. They will dare to
fight them, tho the number of the French
be fuperior. Our feamen of every rank are
at leaft equal to thofe of the French, both
in fkill and courage. Our troops fhew un-
doubted bravery in battle. The intrepidity
of the Britifh officers at the battle of Fon-

* Eftimate, page 141.

tenoy

tenoy has been celebrated by a foreigner *.
It is allowed by the writer of the Eſtimate,
that the French manners are as vain and effeminate as our own †. It is one of his
maxims, that " where effeminacy and ſelf-
" iſh vanity form the ruling character of a
" people, thoſe of high rank and quality
" will, in general, be of all others
" moſt vain, moſt ſelfiſh, moſt incapable,
" moſt effeminate ‡." Why, therefore,
ſhould it be imagined, that French generals, admirals, or miniſters, muſt be ſuperior to Britiſh ?

As there was no juſt ground for admir-
ing the conduct of the French, even when
their affairs appeared moſt proſperous, in the
year 1757; after they had over-run the elec-

* In the Hiſtory of the War of 1741, aſcribed to
Monſieur Voltaire.
This hiſtorian, beſides applauding in general the
courage of the Britiſh troops, obſerves, that in time of
action the officers behaved with great calmneſs and com-
poſure; that they called to the French to fire; that the
troops advanced ſlowly, as if they had been going thro'
their exerciſes; and that the majors were ſeen laying
their canes to the guns of the ſoldiers to cauſe them to
level them in the proper manner. This battle was
fought long within theſe twenty years, during which
period, according to the author of the Eſtimate (page
117) our effeminacy and debility has been ſo much increaſed.

† Eſtimate, page 135.   ‡ Ibid. page 130, 131.

torate

torate of Hanover, and other places in Germany ; their being fhamefully beaten by the gallant king of Pruffia, with fuch inferior numbers ; their winter campaign in Germany ; the want of difcipline among their troops ; their pillaging the countries that were under their power, unlike generous enemies, and contrary to the rules of a fair war ; and their late inglorious flight out of Hanover ; cannot raife our opinion of their councils, generals, or armies, or caufe us to agree more readily with the author of the Eftimate, in his high conceptions of the wifdom, union, military honour, or bravery, of the French nation.

IT is difficult to compare the influence of religion in France and Britain, the fpirit and the principles of it differ fo widely in the two nations. The religion of France leans fo much to fuperftition and to external ceremony ; that of Britain fo much to the pure love of God, and to moral virtue : religion is treated fo differently by the Public in the two nations : the French are fo much overawed by an arbitrary court and a tyrannical clergy ; the Britifh, from the mild fpirit of their government, and from the happy moderation of their clergy, enjoy fo much religious freedom : that in order to determine the force of their religious principles, it is

not

not safe in this, nor indeed, in any other case, to trust solely to *external appearances* of devotion.

As to the *real* quantity of piety and of virtue, it is impossible to *calculate* it at any time. At one time external appearances may be very decent ; there may be great gravity and solemnity in *the looks* ; the outward forms of devotion may be observed with zeal, while religion has not taken firm possession of *the heart*. That sort of religion which flourished during the reign of Charles I. when, to the great disquiet of the nation, the influence of the court was exerted to support and to impose modes and ceremonies in worship, is not much applauded by any party at present. Nor do we admire that enthusiasm, which prevailed under the administration of Oliver Cromwel. It is common now-a-days to represent such flaming appearances of zeal as hypocritical. On the other hand, it is certain, that there may be many lively sentiments of piety in the heart, under a less religious appearance. So that it is, perhaps in truth, more than any man can determine, whether there is not in Britain, at present, as much *real piety and virtue*, as were in it at any point of time since the Reformation. If the impressions of religion seldom appear so fervent in the present age,

they

they seem to be more univerſal, than in former periods.   Mankind often mean well,
even when their external appearance is not
irreproachable.   They may inwardly love
piety and virtue, and may obſerve the more
important duties of life, at the ſame time
that they comply too much with the looſer
modes and faſhions in things eſteemed leſs
ſubſtantial. What is by ſome imputed to vanity, to luxury, and to ſelfiſh effeminacy,
may often, no doubt, be attributed to a ſocial taſte, to a friendly diſpoſition, or to love
of elegance improperly diſplayed.   As the
appearances of piety and virtue under a gra-
ver form are ſometimes hypocritical, ſo when
the better ſort of a nation are not profligate,
nor abandoned to wickedneſs, which is confeſſed to be the caſe at preſent *, amidſt luxury and refined ſenſuality there may be more
ſolid piety and virtue, than is commonly
believed.

The writer of the Eſtimate hath been too
haſty in his cenſure of lord Verulam. " Lord
" Verulam (ſays he) hath ſomewhere ob-
" ſerved, that *times of atheiſm are civil*
" *times.* He had been much nearer the
" truth had he affirmed that *civil times were*
" *times of atheiſm.* He miſtook the cauſe
" for the effect †. "   It hath eſcaped this

* Eſtimate, page 26.   † Ibid. page 165.

writer,

writer, that lord Verulam hath made this very observation. " Learned ages (says this great " philosopher) especially if peaceable and " prosperous, are reckoned among the causes " of atheism ‡." If this observation is just, it may help in some measure to account for that impiety, which is complained of in the present age. For, notwithstanding the complaints made by the author of the Estimate * ; notwithstanding all its defects, the present must be allowed to be a *learned* age. But be this as it will, the great lord Verulam makes another observation, which no religious doctor will deny, that " a smattering of " natural philosophy inclines men to athe- " ism, when a deeper knowledge of nature " brings them about to religion †." Whence

‡ Causæ atheismi sunt : divisiones circa religionem, si plures fuerint; nam unica divisio zelum utriusque partis adauget : verum numerosæ atheismum introducunt. Alia causa sunt scandala sacerdotum ; cum eo res redeat quo innuit S. Bernardus ; Non est jam dicere, Ut populus, sic sacerdos ; quia nec sic populus ut sacerdos. Tertia est, consuetudo profana ludendi et jocandi in rebus sanctis, quæ sensim reverentiam religionis atterit. Postremo ponuntur, secula erudita, præsertim cum pace et rebus prosperis conjuncta.
Verulam. Sermones fideles, De atheismo.
* Estimate, page 41, 42, 43, 86.
† Verum est tamen, parum philosophiæ naturalis homines inclinare in atheismum, at altiorem scientiam eos ad religionem circumagere. *Verulam. Ibid.*
Quin potius certissimum est, atque experientia comprobatum, leves gustus in philosophia movere fortasse ad

we may conclude, notwithſtanding the complaints of the irreligion of the times, that, ſince natural philoſophy has been of late remarkably cultivated and improved in Britain, this deeper knowledge has imprinted a deep ſenſe of the Divinity upon the minds of many.

WITHOUT the imputation of bigotry, it may likewiſe be affirmed, that the proteſtant religion may be expected to have at leaſt as powerful an influence in Britain, as popery has in France, to inſpire its votaries with the love of whatever is great or good. It is ſaid, indeed, that " deſpotiſm arms it-" ſelf with terror ; and, by checking the " open and avowed profeſſion, checks, " in a certain degree, the progreſs of im-" piety †." But whatever effects deſpotiſm may have on the *profeſſion* of religion, the eſtabliſhment of freedom muſt have equal or better effects in promoting *real virtue* and *piety.* And, tho "opinion having its courſe" is ſaid to be a " bad diſeaſe," it is confeſſed at the ſame time, that the cure would be fatal *. Whence it may juſtly be maintained, that, notwithſtanding the advantages accruing to religion from the deſpotiſm of France, there may be at leaſt as much real virtue and piety, of conſequence, religious

atheiſmum, ſed pleniores hauſtus ad religionem reducere.   *Verulam. De Augment. Scient. lib.* i.
 † Eſtimate, page 169.   * Ibid. page 170.

prin-

principles may laſt as long, in Britain, as in France ; tho the author of the Eſtimate ſeems to be of another opinion ‡.

He endeavours to ſhew, * that modern Popery is in danger of overwhelming modern Proteſtantiſm. He ſets forth the faſt hold, which the church of Rome takes of its members by the tremenduous penalty it denounces againſt any departure from its principles. He repreſents the active genius and the fiery ſpirit of the Romiſh religion ; the paſſion and fury, with which it inflames its votaries; the advantages, which it derives from the vices of mankind; the aſſiſtance which it receives from the ſecular arm ; the coolneſs and indifference of many proteſtants both in Great Britain and in America; the zeal of the Romiſh prieſts in making proſelytes, and in urging their party to make them ; the ſtrength which this zeal will acquire even from the benevolent paſſions of mankind, on account of the *ſuppoſed* merit of the Popiſh faith; the premiums which are openly given in England to influence converſions to Popery ; the increaſe of the number of Papiſts in Holland : and, to conclude the whole, he ſets before us the preſent combination of the Popiſh powers againſt the

‡ Eſtimate, page 169.
* In his ſecond Volume, page 127.

King

King of Pruffia; a combination which he attributes in a great meafure to bigotry, and to a permanent uniformity of principles, working in our days the fame effects as they did formerly, when the Elector Palatine was driven out of his dominions.

THUS, he warns us of our danger, and tho, perhaps, every good Proteftant may not fee it in fo ftrong a light, or be as much alarmed as this writer, he will undoubtedly join with him, moft heartily, in his inference, " That we ought to be moft watch- " ful in the prefervation of the invaluable " bleffing of Proteftantifm, and active in " the fupport of thofe who are its great fup- " ports."

SENSIBLE at the fame time, that nothing can fo much quench our ardour as defpondency, he exprefsly cautions againft it, and obferves, that the danger from popery ought to ftrike us only with awe, not with defpondency. To roufe our courage he difplays the great perfonal abilities and fuccefs of the King of Pruffia, whofe remarkable victories ought furely to give great joy to every true Proteftant and true Briton.

BUT, befides that confidence, which may arife from particular alliances, or from the

wifdom

wifdom and valour of a fingle man; if we confider either the matter or the form of the two religions, and the prefent ftate and temper of Chriftendom, the Proteftant religion will appear to have fome very material advantages, and Popery to be expofed to many dangers; from which, as they arife out of its peculiar fyftem, Proteftantifm feems to be altogether fecure.

In the ftruggle betwixt thefe two fyftems, it cannot but be of great benefit to Proteftantifm, that truth and reafon are on its fide. 'Tis true, they do not prevail in every cafe. Yet, as it is always an advantage to have a good caufe, fo in a long conteft the truth and reafon, that are to be found in Proteftantifm, may well be expected to prove a match, if not an over-match, for the falfehood, impoftures, nonfenfe, fuperftition, blind, paffionate and furious zeal, which are fo remarkable in Popery.

Besides the internal weaknefs of Popery, feveral external accidents may happen in the ordinary courfe of affairs, as the refult of caufes which are deeply founded in the nature of man; and may gradually pave the way for the deftruction of Popery.

Not-

NOTWITHSTANDING the religious zeal, which may be obferved in Popifh countries, it is vifible, there is often an inclination in the Princes, as well as others, of the communion of the Church of Rome, to feize part of the exorbitant revenues of the Clergy, and either to add them to their own revenues, or to employ them in encouraging trade and manufactures, to which of late moft of the nations in Europe feem to be greatly turned. There is likewife a difpofition in many of the better fort of the Laity to curb the tyranny of the Priefts, and to prevent their impofitions upon the people. A ftrong fpirit of this kind has appeared lately, and ftill fubfifts in France; and, as it is a *natural* confequence of that *light*, which has been diffufed by the *Reformation* even over the Popifh countries, it may be expected to increafe. In an age, in which fuch a focial intercourfe is eftablifhed betwixt Popifh and Proteftant nations, and fo much knowledge is propagated from fome of them to others, it will be difficult for the Romifh priefts to prevent the confequences of this free communication and increafe of knowledge. The effects of it are felt already. If there are among the Great many Proteftants, who are cool or indifferent about religion, there are many Papifts in the fame rank as indifferent on their fide. In a learned, critical, and

incredulous

incredulous age, fome falfe miracles, of which they are ftill obliged to fupport the credit, will do them much mifchief one time or another. Contefts about privileges muft naturally arife betwixt the Popifh Princes and the Ecclefiaftics. In thofe difputes, notwithftanding the deepeft and moft crafty policy of the conclave, the Clergy will generally be obliged to yield. This will gradually weaken the power of the Church, and at laft be fatal to popery. Popery is not fuch an impregnable fyftem, as is imagined by many. Proteftants have no reafon to think their caufe defperate, but ought to go on courageoufly in the ftruggles with this myftery of iniquity.

As for Great Britain and Ireland, in particular, tho the author of the Eftimate hath affured us, that there is in England one Gentleman who openly gives five pounds to every profelyte to the Roman church, befides the additional bribe of a Sunday's dinner to every fuch perfon as attends mafs, and that allurements of the fame kind are known to prevail in moft parts of the kingdom, and that even among thofe of the higheft rank, a fact, in which, it is hoped, he may be miftaken; tho he might have added, what feems to be of much greater confequence, that there is a greater number of

Papifts

Papiſts than Proteſtants in Ireland ; yet the apprehenſion of loſing the revenues of the antient popiſh church, which are now in the poſſeſſion of Proteſtants ; the excluſion of papiſts from all places of power or profit, while they are ſuffered to live privately in eaſe and quiet ; the riſk, which they muſt run, if they were to attempt any thing againſt the Proteſtant religion ; and the general calmneſs and ſocial ſpirit of our times, promiſe a greater ſecurity to Proteſtantiſm within the King's dominions, than the zeal of the prieſts, or of a few of the laity, or any number of proſelytes, who can be ſuppoſed to be gained to Popery in England, among the loweſt of the people, by bribes of five pounds, and of Sunday dinners, can reaſonably be apprehended to counterbalance.

IT ought indeed to be lamented, that Popery can be ſuppoſed to be increaſing in any part of Britain. Its growth ought to be prevented by all honeſt and lawful means. The miniſters of religion, in particular, ought to lay it ſeriouſly to heart. By a rational and pious zeal in behalf of ſo pure and virtuous a *religion*, as the proteſtant, they will not only do great ſervice to mankind, but recommend themſelves to the eſteem of the world, and reſcue their character and order

from

from any contempt that can be fuppofed to be thrown upon it.

GREAT complaints have, indeed, been made by the author of the Eftimate, as if the clergy were much contemned. Perhaps fuch complaints do not come with the greateft propriety from gentlemen of this order. The decency in which many of them live; the dignity which they maintain; the character which they are well entitled to poffefs; thefe will ever prevent the order itfelf from falling into contempt. Complaints of this kind by clergymen ought always to be diftinguifhed by the modefty with which they are made, as well as by the juftice which accompanies them. It will often, no doubt, be fully as proper to leave them to be made by the laity; from whom they are in a peculiar manner graceful, and may be fuppofed to come with as happy an influence. But whether they come from the one or the other, they are, in fome meafure, juft. The Clergy are furely *lefs* refpected than they *ought to be*. Worthy clergymen are too often contemned by fuch as are neither fo good, nor fo wife, as themfelves. Yet it can fcarce be admitted, that this contempt is fo general, as the author of the Eftimate apprehends. Indeed, if the greateft part of them refemble thofe politer

ones,

ones, among whom, he fays, " it is grown
" a fafhionable thing to defpife the duties of
" their parifh, to wander about, as the va-
" rious feafons invite, to every fcene of falfe
" gaiety, to frequent and fhine in all public
" places, their own pulpits excepted ; or, if
" their age and fituation fet them above
" thefe puerile amufements, they flumber in
" a ftall, haunt levees, or follow the gain-
" ful trade of election-jobbing * ; " we
need not wonder that they are contemned by
both good and bad. But, it is to be hoped,
there are only a few who deferve this character. It is to be hoped, that the writer has
been mifled by one or two examples, with
which he has unfortunately happened to be
acquainted, to be too fevere upon this order,
as well as on other profeffions ; and that the
generality of the clergy both are, and deferve
to be, honoured and refpected. Notwithftanding the ftrongeft efforts of fceptics and
freethinkers, it is probable the clergy will
not fall into general contempt. Indeed,
fuch as are vicious ; fuch as in a free proteftant country fet up too high claims to authority in matters of religion ; fuch as demand too great regard *merely* on account of
their *gown and band* : or fuch as are *con-
ceited, proud, infolent,* and *overbearing,* and

* Eftimate, page 84, 85.

allow

allow no virtue in *any man* who will not *blindly submit to their order*, may, perhaps, be defpifed. And, if men of fo exceptionable a character fhould be much contemned, it is none of the worft figns of an age. It is not furely a proof, either that the profeffion of a clergyman is generally contemned, or that religion has loft its influence in the world. But to proceed.

THE author of the Eftimate will needs maintain, that tho the manners of the French are as vain, as felfifh, and as effeminate, as thofe of the Britifh, the French have greatly the advantage of us in refpect of national defence. And for this he offers his reafons. But, on examination, thefe reafons will be found weak ; and fome of them muft *found odly* in the ears of a true Briton.

FIRST we are told, that the effeminacy of the French does not, like that of the Britifh, affect their national capacity ; becaufe their " youth are affiduoufly trained up for all " public offices, civil, naval, military, in " fchools provided at the public expence, and " the candidates for public employ go thro' " a fevere and laborious courfe of difci- " pline *."

* Eftimate, page 135, 136.

THAT

THAT there are such schools in France, and that they are on a better footing than any of the same kind in Britain, will not, perhaps, be denied. Nor will any impartial man maintain, that the French do not discover a superior skill in several branches of their police. But tho one should be willing to do them justice, it is hardly possible to avoid observing, that the writer of the Estimate lays a greater weight upon the institution of their schools, than it will bear.

In a nation where the manners are vain and effeminate, it is scarce to be thought that the youth of better fashion will be obliged to go through a very severe and laborious course of discipline; at least, that any course of discipline, through which they can be supposed to go when they are young, will be able to prevent the bad effects of effeminate manners, with which they are surrounded as soon as they appear in the world. In fact, the extraordinary effects of this severe discipline are seldom to be felt by experience. The British will meet the French with equal numbers either by sea or by land.

No doubt, a course of proper discipline, such as we read of during some periods among some of the ancient nations, the Spartans, for instance, and the Romans, will do much to

inspire

infpire valour and patriotifm. But we have no reafon to entertain the fame high opinion of a French education. A vain, luxurious, felfifh, and effeminate people can fcarce be fuppofed capable of directing a proper education : nor can their country be a proper fcene for it. French education is certainly very defective. But tho it were better than it is, it is not *fufficient* for fitting the youth to be generals, admirals, or minifters of ftate. When we fearch after proper perfons to direct public councils, or to command armies and fleets (and this is what the author of the Eftimate is in queft of) we fhall find that a French education goes but a little way towards forming them. In truth, it is not education, it is nature, which muft qualify men for fuch important offices. Educate a coward, or a filly man, how you will, you will never make him a Marlborough. In order to make a ftatefman or a general, befides genius, honefty, activity, and courage, obfervation and experience are neceffary. If our countrymen behave ill, it is not becaufe in general we are worfe educated than the French : our bad behaviour ought to be imputed to caufes which operate on them as much as on us.

2. IT is pleafant to find it given as another reafon, why the effeminacy of the
French

French manners affects not their national capacity, that " the youth in France only ex-
" pect to rife in ftation, as they rife in
" knowledge and ability *." Perhaps the
Britifh youth form the fame expectations.
One may venture to fay, they have as good
reafon to do fo. But the French as well as
the Englifh youth will find themfelves difappointed, when they come out into the
world. The kings of France cannot, any
more than thofe of Britain, fee every thing
with their own eyes. It will be impoffible
for them to know the perfonal merit of every
one they employ. They muft truft to their
minifters. If the manners of the court of
France are, as they are confeffed to be, as
vain and effeminate as thofe of the court of
Britain, why fhould not the caprice of a favourite, the affection of a minifter for his
relations and friends, the intrigues he muft enter into to fupport himfelf againft the plots
of his rivals, or even indolence, floth, and
luxury, as often pervert his choice in procuring commiffions and offices, as the like
caufes will pervert a minifter in England ?
It is faid the power of our parliaments gives
rife to dangerous factions in Britain. But
there may be, nay, in truth there are, as
violent factions, as bafe and unmanly in-

* Eftimate, page 136,

trigues,

trigues, in order to obtain the good graces of a king of France, as there can be in Britain to obtain a parliamentary interest, and recommendations to favour. In fact, it will be found, that there are as foolish and as unworthy promotions in the one country as in the other.

AGAIN, 3. the warlike spirit of the French nobility, and the principle of military honour, are said to prevent the dangerous effects of their effeminate manners. " Tho " commerce (says the author of the Esti- " mate) is encouraged in France, it is chiefly " encouraged among the commons: while the " people are allured to trade by every kind " of motive, and allowed to reap the chief " profits of it, the noblesse or gentry are in " honour prohibited from commerce *. " The leading ranks in France are not so rich, as in England; and, being discouraged from trading, their poverty drives them to the profession of arms as the necessary means of support †. Hence the French are both a commercial and a warlike nation. The effeminacy of their manners is corrected, and the danger arising from it much prevented, by the greater remainder of military genius.

* Estimate, page 205.   † Ibid. page 204.

IN this reprefentation there are fome things, which cannot be contefted. Indeed, the Britifh reckon themfelves happy, that they cannot difpute the truth of them. The gentlemen of France go into the army more frequently, than the gentry in England. The Englifh are not under the fame neceffity as the French : the gentry and nobility are rich, and the profeffion of a merchant is honourable among the former. No miniftry nor favourite of the king can make them uneafy, tho they live at home upon their eftates, and neither go themfelves nor fend any of their family to the court or to the army. The French noblefle are poor. It is reckoned difhonourable for them to trade. Should they decline going to the court, or entering into the army, the court has many methods of diftreffing them. So they muft fly to the army for their fupport and protection. But this does not render a French fuperior to a Britifh army. Indeed, the Britifh ought rather to be preferred, fince its leaders are not more felfifh, more vain, or more effeminate, than thofe of the French; and the private men in the Britifh fervice muft be confeffed to be better, the commons in Britain being at leaft equally courageous, and generally more robuft and high-fpirited, than thofe of France.

THERE is another refpect, indeed, in which

which the French have the advantage. Their armies are more numerous ; and to this, rather than to any superior bravery, their success in the late war is to be ascribed. In this respect it is not proposed to make a comparison. The British will yield to their rivals the honour of having such great armies : they prefer the arts of peace : their Government consults their happiness, and does not, like the French, employ them in frequent wars without necessity *. The great armies in France are a heavy burden upon the people ; the British, being surrounded by the sea, stand not in need of such defenders : but if at any time the Government wants an army, it is able to raise one, and abundance of the nobility and gentry are ready to court military employments, and fairly to dispute the honours of the field with any of the armies of France.

4. If the French, therefore, are better secured, than the British, against the danger of their vain and effeminate manners, it must chiefly be by the despotic power of the king. It is this, which, according to the author of the Estimate, aided by the principle of military honour, secures the natural spirit of union. The monarch's power gives unity

* Estimate, page 205.

and fteadinefs to every movement of the ftate *. In a country where freedom is eftablifhed, and manners loft through the exorbitance of wealth, the duration of religious principles can be but fhort. Defpotifm arms itfelf with terror; and, by checking the open and avowed profeffion, checks, in a certain degree, the progrefs of impiety: whereas it muft be acknowledged and lamented as one of the unalterable defects of a free government, that opinion muft have its courfe †. The national fpirit of union is naturally ftrong in abfolute monarchies: in free countries it is naturally weak ‡. The reftraints laid on the royal prerogative at the Revolution, and the acceffion of liberty thus gained by the people, added to our parliaments a new dignity and power. Hence the members, fenfible of their influence, make demands on the crown; and the conftituents, fenfible of their influence, make demands on their reprefentatives. Thus the loweft cobler preffes on the minifter. If the different claimants are vefted with lucrative employments, the wheels of government run fmooth. If any large body of claimants are diffatisfied, the political uproar begins, and public meafures are obftructed or overturned. Thus the grand chain of political inter-

* Eftimate, page 140.   † Ibid. page 169, 170.
‡ Ibid. page 103,

eft

eſt has been formed. The origin of making parliaments is to be traced from the reign of king William III. but the art at that time was but in its infancy. The ſyſtem gathered ſtrength by degrees. The grand chain of political ſelf-intereſt has been at length compleated, and a foundation laid in our principles and manners for endleſs diſſentions in the ſtate. Thus, faction is eſtabliſhed among us. But theſe miſchiefs are much prevented in France by the deſpotic power of the monarch *. In this manner does the author of the Eſtimate ſet forth the diſadvantages of Britiſh freedom, and the advantages of deſpotic power in France.

Of one thing, however, ſo far as I have obſerved, he hath omitted to take notice, namely, that the exorbitant trade and wealth, which he confeſſes we poſſeſs at preſent †, are owing to the ſecurity and liberty, which the nation gained at the Revolution above what they had enjoyed in the preceding period. Tho this did not occur to this writer, it is, indeed, the truth. And by adding this circumſtance to thoſe which he hath obſerved, the ſeries will ſtand connected as follows : By the Revolution we have gained

* Eſtimate, page 107—123. † Ibid. page 209.

ſecurity

security and *liberty* : security and liberty have produced an *exorbitant trade and wealth* : this wealth hath very near deftroyed the principles of religion, honour, and public fpirit, and hath prodigioufly corrupted our manners. Bad manners, when there is nothing fufficient to give check to their natural confequences, muft firft enervate, and then ruin, a nation. One of thefe principal checks is the defpotic power of the king. This has a happy effect in France, to fecure the nation againft the dangers arifing from their luxury and effeminacy. We have not this advantage in Britain. Formerly our kings had certain prerogatives, which might have been ufeful in this refpect ; but we have loft thefe advantages fince the Revolution, by the reftraints which were laid on the royal prerogative at that time. Hence, there being now nothing in our conftitution to give due check to our bad manners, their natural confequences muft have their full effect, and we run the greateft rifk of going to deftruction. This feems to be the ftate of the cafe, according to the writer of the Eftimate.

In all this I am far from accufing this gentleman of any intention to caft black and odious colours on the Revolution, or of being unfriendly to the dignity and powers of our parliaments, and to the liberty of the

people

people of Britain. I only take notice of the *confequences* of certain principles, but fhall be far from fuppofing the writer was fenfible of thefe confequences. An author, out of love to his country, and from an honeft indignation againft the depravity of its manners, in affigning the fources of this depravity may unawares fuffer expreffions to drop from his pen, which may bear hard upon that very fyftem which himfelf efpoufes. It is not uncommon even for doctors to write inconfiftently, and to lay down pofitions, from which dangerous confequences may fairly be inferred. But in moft cafes, it is unfair to impute to any man confequences which he does not acknowledge, or which are contrary to his open declarations. Such an imputation cannot but do harm both to the man who is guilty of it, and to the caufe which he defends.

The writer of the Eftimate applauds the fpirit of liberty, and the ftruggles it maintained formerly with the tyrants of the times *. He allows the rebellion in the year 1745 to have been mifchievous † ; acknowledges, that the friends of liberty are

* Eftimate, p. 18.   † Ibid. page 92.

the

the friends of Britain ‡ ; and confesses, that our constitution is of a superior nature to that of France *.　Out of affection and regard to such a constitution, tho he thinks "opinion's " having a free course" is a " bad disease," yet he declares against any attempt to cure the disease, because it is an unalterable defect of a free government †.　Tho he has conceived a bad opinion of the present age, and formed the most frightful ideas of the dangers arising from a free government, except in simple and virtuous times ‡,　yet he declares for a free government even in our degenerate times.

Thus, he appears a *generous* friend to liberty, and a determined enemy to despotism, At the same time he is greatly mistaken concerning the dangers which he supposes to arise from the one, and the blessed effects which he ascribes to the other.

Of all this gentleman's errors, this is surely the most unlucky and the most dangerous.　He hath fallen into other mistakes. There are few professions, perhaps, to which he hath wholly done justice.　In general, he is too severe in his reproofs : but such er-

‡ Estimate, p. 91.　　* Ibid. p. 218.
† Ibid. p. 170.　　‡ Ibid. p. 1c8.

rors

rors are more harmlefs ; they may even be attended with fome accidental benefit. If fuch exaggerated reprefentations of vicious and effeminate manners do not drive the nation to defpair, they may ferve to awaken it. No benefit, indeed, can arife from the advantageous light in which he places French councils and generals. This rather tends to intimidate our armies in time of war. Yet it is probable it will do little harm, as our foldiers, not acknowledging the fuperiority of the French, will not truft to his opinion, nor be frighted by romantic difplays of French heroifm. But the views which he he gives his countrymen, of the dangers arifing from liberty, and of the advantages of the French defpotifm, not only tend to excite a diftafte of liberty, to reconcile the minds of the people to defpotic power, an to beget an admiration of abfolute monarchy in general, but may, in particular, be expected to have a bad influence at this time, if the nation fhall fuffer any confiderable loffes in the prefent war. It is neceffary, therefore, to expofe fuch a dangerous miftake, and to provide an antidote againft the fatal poifon.

IT is true, if this gentleman's affertions concerning the confequences of liberty and defpotifm are found, there is no help for it.

We

We muſt ſtand to them. But happily this is not the caſe, and the writer's ideas on this ſubject are wholly viſionary.

FOR what reaſon ſhould it be thought, that, except in virtuous times, the power and dignity of parliaments, and the liberty of the people, muſt be ſo dangerous, and that deſpotic power in the prince muſt be ſo uſeful to prevent the bad conſequences of effeminate manners, ſince this effeminacy has at leaſt as great influence on the prince and his power, as on any thing elſe? Effeminacy muſt principally affect thoſe in higher life. It eſpecially infects the court and the officers of the army. The prince cannot ſee every thing with his own eyes : he cannot govern entirely by himſelf : he muſt be informed by his courtiers : his meaſures muſt be much directed by his miniſters. The manners of theſe gentlemen, it is confeſſed, are vain, ſelfiſh, and effeminate. This muſt corrupt their ſchemes and adminiſtration. The power of the king, be it ever ſo great, muſt be employed to ſupport and execute the effeminate and ſelfiſh ſchemes of an effeminate and ſelfiſh miniſtry. Why, therefore, ſhould the king's *deſpotic* power give ſo great ſecurity againſt the bad conſequences of ſelfiſh and effeminate manners? Inſtead of giving check to the evil, deſpotic power tends much ra

ther

ther to prevent all hopes or poffibility of a remedy to fuch a dangerous malady.

In the conftitution of France there are not any effectual refources in a ftate of corruption. The king's abfolute power crufhes all who oppofe the foolifh and pernicious projects of his corrupted minifters. The Britifh conftitution has a manifeft advantage in this refpect. Corruption may creep in among the people; it may gather ftrength by degrees. Times of inward peace, opulence, and fecurity, fuch as we have enjoyed fince the Revolution, may unfortunately carry this corruption to a great height. The love of money is the root of all evil *. Too high a value for life, and too fmall a fenfe of honour, are equally bafe and dangerous. It muft be confeffed, all the three prevail too much at prefent. Corruption, no doubt, may rife fo high, as to overpower whatever would refift it. Thus, no nation, no conftitution is abfolutely fecure. But, if there are effectual remedies againft deftruction in any, they are to be found in the Britifh, conftitution. In France there is nothing that can make head againft the wicked intentions, deftructive negligence, or fatal ftupidity of a wicked and effeminate court. But in Bri-

* 1 Timothy, vi. 10.

tain

tain the voice of the middle ranks among the people has a mighty influence. These are always the last to be corrupted. In their integrity and activity there is a grand resource. When those in higher life are sunk in depravity and effeminacy, if there is any genius or honesty left in the nation, and scarce can any civilized people be supposed wholly destitute of either of them, the cry and influence of this part of the people will often be able to find them out and bring them into play. Our constitution, therefore, having such a high mixture of freedom, is better fitted, than the despotism of France, to preserve us from destruction.

But, God be thanked! there is no necessity to have recourse to extraordinary remedies. Our most gracious sovereign, who is so justly beloved by his people, with the assistance of the legislature, is fully able to support the nation against the power of France. The brave and virtuous part of the people ought not to lose their courage, or to despair of the cause of their country.

The nation (says the author of the Estimate) " stands aghast at its own misfortunes ; but, like a man starting suddenly from sleep by the noise of some approaching ruin, knows neither whence
" it

" it comes, nor how to avoid it ‡." Here we have a lively image; the simile is fine; nothing is wanting but solidity. One would think the French had not only made themselves masters of the plains of America, but had beat us on the plains of Salisbury, and were marching fast to London to pillage a defenceless capital *. But, in place of such remarkable defeats, hitherto, if the advantage is not on our side, the losses are pretty equally balanced between the two nations †, that of Minorca alone excepted. By the loss of this important island, the conquest of our forefathers since the Revolution, we have not only lost an useful station for our ships, but, which is of greater moment, have suf-

‡ Estimate, page 149, 150.

* The author of the Estimate seems apprehensive of some such event. He ought not to be blamed. Would to God, every Britain was awakened out of security, and believed a French invasion and the rout of a British army in Britain, events that are far from being impossible; and from a sense of this would submit to every measure proper to prevent the danger. Then should we be as safe against all foreign invasions, as we are now from internal commotions.

† If it be true, as seems very probable, that we have greatly hurt the French trade; that the insurance upon French ships is very high; that the French finances are much incumbered; and that the French government cannot borrow money for double of the interest, at which our government may have it in Britain; the advantage, perhaps, will be found on our side, notwithstanding the loss of Minorca, and of some of our forts and back settlements in America.

fered

fered in our national honour. Yet there is no reason why we should despond, or apprehend universal ruin. Excepting the case of Minorca, we have been rather *disappointed* in our expectations of success against the enemy, than met with any considerable defeat or actual calamity.

In religion, when a sinner despairs of mercy, his condition is desperate : while he sinks under the weight of his sins, he is incapable of repentance. There is a resemblance in the condition of a whole people. To aggravate national calamities, national vices, or national weaknesses, does not become a patriot. It is nobler far, and more useful, for the people of Britain to imitate the firmness and magnanimity of the Roman state. After the entire destruction of their army at the battle of Cannæ (a misfortune so great, that nothing but the total rout of a British by a French army near the metropolis of the island could be compared to it) this magnanimous people thanked their consul, that he had not despaired of the common-wealth *. To promote such a cou-

---

* Nec tamen hæ clades defectionesque sociorum moverunt ut pacis unquam mentio apud Romanos fieret ; neque ante consulis Romam adventum, nec postquam is rediit, renovavitque memoriam acceptæ cladis. Quo in tempore ipso adeo magno animo civitas fuit, ut con-

rageous

rageous ſpirit, to prevent a baleful deſpon-
dency, and not to juſtify any ill-concerted

ſuli, ex tanta clade, cujus ipſe cauſa maxima fuiſſet,
redeunti, et obvium itum frequenter ab omnibus ordi-
nibus ſit, et gratiæ actæ quod de republica non deſpe-
raſſet. *Tit. Liv. Lib.* xxii. *c. p.* 61.

There were ſome, however, among that courageous
people, who, ſtruck with the greatneſs of the calamity,
and deſpairing of being able to defend their country
againſt the ſuperior genius of Hannibal and the Cartha-
ginians, were deliberating about abandoning Italy, and
about ſheltering themſelves ingloriouſly in the territories
of ſome of the neighbouring monarchs ; preferring a
mean, ſlaviſh, and precarious life, under a ty ant, to
freedom, or a glorious death in defence of their country. But the brave Scipio ſoon put an end to ſuch
cowardly reſolutions. The account is from Livy, and
deſerves to be read in the beautiful original.

Quibus conſultantibus inter paucos de ſumma rerum
nunciat P. Furius Philus conſularis viri filius ; " Ne-
" quicquam eos perditam ſpem fovere : deſperatam
" comploratamque rem eſſe publicam. Nobiles juve-
" nes quoſdam, quorum principem L. Cæcilium Me-
" tellum, mare et naves ſpectare, ut, deſerta Italia, ad
" regum aliquem transfugerent." Quqd malum, præ-
terquam atrox, ſuper tot clades etiam novum, quum
ſtupore et miraculo torpidos defixiſſet, et, qui aderant
concilium advocandum cenſerent ; negat concilii rem
eſſe Scipio juvenis, fatalis dux hujuſce belli. " Auden-
" dum atque agendum, non conſultandum, ait, in tan-
" to malo eſſe. Irent ſecum extemplo armati, qui rem-
" publicam ſalvam vellent. Nullo verius, quam ubi ea
" cogitentur, hoſtium caſtra eſſe " Pergit ire, ſequen-
tibus paucis, in hoſpitium Metelli. Et quum concilium
ibi juvenum, de quibus allatum erat, inveniſſet, ſtricto
ſuper capita conſultantium gladio, " Ex mei animi ſen-
" tentia," inquit, " ut ego rempublicam populi Ro-

puſil-

pusillanimous measures or conduct, hath the author of these characteristics taken upon him to offer some reflections on the state of the Public.

AT the same time he will be far from either deluding or seducing the people, and saying " Peace, peace, where there is no " peace *. As with lies he will not make " the heart of the righteous sad, whom God " hath not made sad, so neither will he " strengthen the hands of the wicked, " that he should not return from his " wicked way, by promising him life †." God knows, there is enough of irreligion, luxury, vanity, selfish effeminacy, stupidity, and cowardice, to awaken the concern of every true patriot, and to shew the necessity of correcting our errors. Especially those of higher rank ought to exert themselves to recover their own honour and the

" mani non deferam, neque alium civem Romanum de-
" ferere patiar. Si sciens fallo, tum me, Jupiter Optime
" Maxime, domum, familiam, remque meam pessimo
" leto afficias! In hæc verba, L. Cæcili, jures, pos-
" tulo, cæterque, qui adestis : qui non juraverit, in se
" hunc gladium strictum esse sciat." Haud secus pavidi, quam si victorem Hannibalem cernerent, jurant omnes : custodiendosque semetipsos Scipioni tradunt.
Tit. Liv. Lib. xxii. *cap.* 53.

* Ezekiel, xiii. 10.
† Ezekiel, xiii. 22.

honour

honour of the nation. From the Eſtimate, which has gone through ſo many editions, and from other writings, they may learn, how multitudes are diſpoſed to think of their conduct. Would they retrieve their character, would they regain the good opinion of their country, they muſt make a vigorous uſe of the riches and ſtrength of the nation. The time is not too late. Tho engaged in a war againſt a powerful enemy, we have many reſources. Great as the power of France muſt be acknowledged to be, it muſt be much greater than it is ; effeminate as we are repreſented, we muſt be much more effeminate than we are, before the French can expect to conquer this iſland. The Britiſh ought not to deſpiſe their enemy. Yet when we conſider our ſituation, in an iſland, the greatneſs of our naval power, that our enemies dare hardly ever meet us in open ſea, can only infeſt our trade by privateering, and are obliged to ſteal their ſhips of war out of their harbours at ſuch times as they may hope to eſcape our ſuperior ſquadrons : when we conſider that our iſland affords us all the neceſſaries of life in great abundance ; that by domeſtic induſtry and foreign commerce we have acquired money, that is, the ſinews of war, and are poſſeſſed of plenty of arms, and all kinds of military and naval ſtores ; that we are upon a reſpectable footing

ing in the Eaſt Indies, and that our colonies in America are far ſuperior to thoſe of the French in wealth and numbers of people: when we conſider that there are more than two millions of men in Britain as robuſt and high ſpirited as any in Europe; that Britiſh ſeamen in general are at leaſt equal, if not ſuperior to the French; that a body of commanders can be drawn out of our nobility and gentry not more effeminate than their rivals, equal to them in honour, public ſpirit, and valour: in fine, when it is conſidered, that, whatever ſmaller diviſions there are among us, we will unite againſt the French, under a King of known juſtice and courage, beloved by his people, ready to gratify their deſires, and to comply with the propoſals made him by his parliament; ſo many advantages, in a naval war, create a juſt confidence, that, notwithſtanding ſome diſappointments to our juſt expectations at the beginning of it, the ſuperiority will at laſt be found to be greatly on our ſide.

To all the advantages already mentioned, I ſhall add another, which is of the greateſt conſequence; and with it I ſhall conclude all that I intended. The French are all ſubjected to the deſpotic, uncontroulable power of an arbitrary monarch. We are free under the protection of law. Inſtead of

looking

looking on defpotifm as an advantage to them, or on freedom as a difadvantage to us, we ought to account our liberty as a mighty advantage on our fide both in peace and in war.

I shall not enlarge on the fuperior influence of freedom in promoting arts and fciences, in advancing learning and philofophy, and in encouraging commerce and agriculture. This has been fo well and fo often explained, that it is now generally confeffed by all forts of writers. I fhall only take notice in general, that, if we confider the *nature* and *internal conftitution* of free governments, and compare them with defpotic monarchies, it will appear, that free ftates are the only proper nurferies of arts and fciences, and that it is fcarce poffible they could have arifen under defpotic monarchies *. And, if we confult *experience* and the hiftory of the world, we fhall find, that the arts *actually* arofe under free governments; and that, tho they have been tranfplanted into abfolute monarchies, and have flourifhed in a certain degree under them, both arts and commerce

* See Mr. Hume's Effay on the Rife and Progrefs of Arts and Sciences.

have

have flourished moſt and longeſt in free nations.

IT is more material, in the preſent queſtion, to conſider the influence of freedom
in times of war, and to examine the chances
of a free government againſt an abſolute
monarchy.   To make the compariſon juſt,
we muſt not oppoſe a free government of
the beſt kind to an abſolute monarchy of
the worſt, or a deſpotic monarchy of the
beſt form to the worſt kind of republics;
but muſt ſuppoſe each of them to be the beſt
of its kind, or rather to be as good as hath
exiſted, or can reaſonably be ſuppoſed to
exiſt, in the world, and to be as well governed, and as much free from corruption,
as ſuch a government commonly is.   Without this precaution we cannot make a proper
compariſon.

IN all political queſtions it will be difficult
to lay down general rules which will hold
at all times.   In all events, and in all human affairs, there is ſo great a diſſimila-
rity, that few caſes are exactly alike. Much
will ever depend upon particular circumſtances.   At certain times, either a free or
a deſpotic government may ſuddenly ſubdue
and ſwallow up the other.   A free government may be weak through faction and
luxury,

luxury, while an abſolute monarchy is ſtrong by the force and wiſdom of ſome of its inſtitutions, or by the happy genius of its prince or grand vizir.

But, abſtracting from theſe particular circumſtances, it is eſſential to the idea of every free government, that the power be not wholly veſted in one man, but be diſtributed among different individuals and different bodies of men. By which means each man's condition approaching much nearer to an equality with that of his neighbours, than can be ſuppoſed under an abſolute monarchy, and no man being wholly contemptible, ſuch a government may well be called a government, not of men, but of laws. For general rules, founded on the principles of equity, muſt be eſtabliſhed to regulate the conduct of all the individuals, among whom the adminiſtration is diſtributed. Therefore, under ſuch a conſtitution there neither is, nor indeed can be, ſuch oppreſſion or arbitrary procedure, as under a deſpotic monarchy. Every man is not only ſafer *,

---

* It is ſurpriſing it ſhould be aſſerted, that a ſubject in France is as ſafe as a ſubject in Britain. " Private " property ſeems to me (ſays an ingenious auth or in " his Eſſay of Liberty and Deſpotiſm) fully as ſecure " in a civilized European monarchy, as in a republic. " Nor is any danger apprehended in ſuch a government

but

but may fee that his life, his perfonal liberty, and his property are more fecure, than
under a defpotic monarchy. Hence it will
not only be natural for him to feel a greater
boldnefs and firmnefs of mind, but he has
reafon to conceive that he has a greater intereft in the government, than any man
can have under an abfolute monarchy. He
has ftronger motives to love, fupport, and
fight for his country. The attachments to
the family, the perfon, or the glory of the
Prince cannot be fo powerful under an abfolute monarchy, as the *amor patriæ* under
a free conftitution. Therefore the fubjects
of a free government (cæteris paribus) muft
be *more vigorous and more valiant* than thofe
of an abfolute prince.

" from the violence of the fovereign, no more than we
" commonly apprehend danger from thunder or earth-
" quakes, or any accident the moft unufual and extra-
" ordinary." What may be apprehended, I will not
pretend to fay. Mens fafety does not depend upon
what they may apprehend, but on the real nature of
their condition. One may be in great danger, when
he does not apprehend it. Whether one is in fafety,
muft be determined not from what does, but from what
may, happen. A fubject in France may be merry and
jovial; but he has not an equal fecurity with a fubject
of Britain, of not being thrown into prifon never
more to be heard of. Tho few are ftruck dead with
thunder, yet no man on earth is as fafe from thunder
as if he were above the clouds.

AGAIN

AGAIN, in a free government, little depends on the character and genius either of any one man, or of a few men. Its wise inftitutions, cuftoms, and laws muft be fuppofed more fteady and durable, and confequently more able to form the people to virtue. Whereas, under an abfolute monarchy much will always depend on the genius and abilities of the prince, and of a few of his favourites. A prince, endowed with a mighty genius, may arife; he may be greatly ambitious of true glory, and may be both willing and able to promote the happinefs and grandeur of his people. But, if fuch a monarch had a predeceffor of a different character, or if he is fucceeded by a weak or vicious prince, fo much muft be done during a fingle life, that there will not be fufficient time for training up his fubjects to fo high a degree of virtue, as may be done eafily where the inftitutions are more durable, and where the laws have a more uninterrupted influence. In the common courfe of human affairs, a fucceffion of two or three great men is rarely to be feen in any one family. Hardly can it be expected, that a royal education, in an abfolute monarchy, fhould give a better chance to the families of princes.

If

IF it be faid, that abfolute monarchs have an advantage over republics, becaufe they can keep their counfels more fecret; this will be found more fpecious than folid. Either thofe occafions are very rare, in which an abfolute fecrecy is neceffary for the public fafety; or, if they occur more frequently, free governments are not incapable of all that fecrecy which is needful. A limited royal authority, with certain difcretionary powers and prerogatives in the prince, is not inconfiftent with the higheft freedom. The king may concert the moft important defigns with one man or with a few. The generals of republics may have as great powers as thofe of abfolute monarchs. There is an advantage, no doubt, in many cafes, in a certain degree of fecrecy and caution. However, the wifeft and beft counfels are thofe which need leaft to be concealed; and thofe, who either affect, or need to affect, a myfterious air of fecrecy, are certainly the weakeft politicians.

THO it is a common objection to free governments, that they are liable to factions, yet in matters of the greateft importance they are upon the whole more fteady than abfolute monarchies.

UNDER

UNDER free governments different parties may prevail at different times. One miniftry may come in place of another. Plans of lefs confequence may be altered. Contrary meafures may be purfued. But where the chief interefts of a nation, or its immediate fafety, are at ftake, it will be difficult to conceal this from a free people, or to render them indifferent about their moft important concerns. What tends either to the immediate ruin of a people on the one hand, or, on the other, to render them fecure, is not fo difficult to be underftood, that a great number in a free nation fhould not be capable of difcerning it, and of pointing it out to their fellow-citizens. In a free country, thofe who govern, be they many or be they few, muft have a regard to the *fenfe of the people*, and keep their more important interefts more fteadily in view, than under a government where the voice of the people is lefs fignificant.

INSTEAD, therefore, of concluding, that the counfels of an abfolute monarchy muft be fteady, we may conclude, on the contrary, that, where fo much depends on the fingle opinion or caprice of an arbitrary monarch, or of his prime minifter, ftability of conduct, even in things of the greateft importance, can hardly be expected. The

coun-

counfels in fuch a government muft be fluctuating in their own nature ; for abfolute governments are liable to fudden changes
and violent convulfions.   Under free ones,
the wifdom, virtue, or activity of one man
or party may correct the folly, wickednefs,
or indolence of another ; an advantage, of
which an abfolute monarchy is deprived.   A
wife and an able prince of an active and enter-
prizing temper may fometimes accomplifh
mighty defigns, within his own dominions,
of which he is entirely the mafter.   He may
fometimes give law to his weaker neighbours.
A weak and inactive prince, who fucceeds,
may, if he chances to have an able minifter,
follow the plan that has been laid down by
the greater genius of his predeceffor.   But,
on the whole, the counfels of a defpotic monarchy may be expected to be unftable and
uncertain.

If France be cited as an inftance of the
contrary ; if it be alledged, that this monarchy has purfued a fteady plan for aggrandiz-
ing the nation, ever fince the beginning of
the reign of Lewis XIV. if not from that of
Henry IV. the anfwer is eafy.   It is fuggefted by Mr. Hume * : " If the world is ftill
" too young to fix many general ftable

* Effay of Liberty and Defpotifm.

truths

" truths in politics, which will remain true
" to the lateft pofterity ; if we have not as
" yet had the experience of above three
" thoufand years ; if we want fufficient ma-
" terials upon which we can reafon in the
" fcience of politics; if it is not fully known
" what degrees of refinement, either in vir-
" tue or in vice, human nature is fufceptible
" of, nor what may be expected of man-
" kind from any great revolution in their
" education, cuftoms, or principles ;" much
lefs can we form any certain conclufions
from the appearances of the French monarchy during only an hundred years.

How foon was an end put to all the grand
defigns of Henry IV ! A fatal proof how
little an abfolute monarchy can be depended
on.

Notwithstanding the political adminiftration of cardinal Richelieu, the reign of
Lewis XIII. furnifhes us with little that
was truly great.

It may be doubted, whether Lewis XIV.
notwithftanding all his inftitutions for encouraging commerce, notwithftanding his
great fuccefs in war during forty years, did
not leave France poorer and weaker, than he
found it when he entered on the adminiftration

tion of the government. According to monfieur de Voltaire, who rather writes a panegyric than a hiftory of this prince, before the peace of Utrecht France was drained of men and money. Some parts of it were ravaged by an hoftile army. Verfailles was alarmed as well as the reft of the kingdom. It was debated at court, whether the king fhould retire to Chambort. In fhort, this hiftorian confeffes, that the latter part of the reign of Lewis XIV. was diftinguifhed by calamities *, and that at his death he left debts amounting to one hundred and eighty millions fterling †. So dearly did the French pay for the ambition of this their boafted monarch, and for the victories gained by him during the firft part of his reign.

FRANCE has flourifhed more under his fucceffor, though his genius is not thought fo brilliant as that of Lewis XIV. But how foon may a king of France of a different character from that of Lewis XIV. or of Lewis XV. or a prime minifter the reverfe of Colbert or Fleury, alter the whole face of the French monarchy, and render it as infignificant, as it has lately appeared important, in the fcale of nations. France

---

* Le Siecle de Louis XIV. Tom. i. chap. 22.
† Ibid. Tom. ii. chap. 28.

nar-

narrowly efcaped being difmembered in the reign of queen Anne. The prefent diffentions between its parliaments and the clergy, for the moft defpotic governments cannot prevent parties, may be followed by extraordinary confequences, and excite civil diffentions which no defpotic monarch can pacify. The grandeur of the French monarchy can as little be afcertained, as that of other monarchies, which have flourifhed during a reign or two, and have afterwards funk into feeblenefs and contempt. No nation can be affured of eternal empire. All our conjectures concerning fuch fubjects muft be extremely uncertain. But if we will examine probabilities, Britain, whether we confider its government, or its fituation, bids fairer, than any other, for duration.

If we confult the hiftory of the world, the power and firmnefs of free governments, and the weaknefs of defpotic monarchies, will appear more manifeft. The free ftates of Greece overthrew the huge armies of Xerxes, and preferved their greatnefs againft all the power of the Perfian monarchs. Thofe defpotic princes, who were mafters of fuch extenfive dominions, and commanded fo many millions of people, did not think themfelves fafe from the power of the Greeks as long as
they

they purfued one common intereft. It was, therefore, the policy of the Perfian monarchs, by the force of money and by intrigues, to excite quarrels, and to fow jealoufies among the Grecian ftates, that they might not unite to attack the Perfian empire. In this dif-jointed condition, Philip of Macedon gain-ed fome advantages over the Greeks, and broke their ftrength in fome degree. But this Philip of Macedon was not an abfolute monarch. The Macedonians were confider-ed as *free* men. Their condition was cer-tainly very different from that of the Per-fians and the other Afiatics, who lived un-der defpotic monarchs. Befides, Philip ne-ver pretended to an abfolute conqueft of the Greek ftates. He rather affected to be their protector, and their general againft the Per-fians, than their king. He did not weaken them fo fully, as not to be defpifed by the Lacedemonians in the midft of his glory *. His fon Alexander was a great conqueror : but, as he was not a defpotic monarch, fo he fought not againft free nations, but againft defpotic monarchs and their flaves. The

* When he had called all the ftates of Greece to fend deputies to Corinth, the Lacedemonians defpifed his meffage. Lacedæmonii et legem et regem contem-pferunt. Justin, lib. ix. cap. 5.

single

single city of Tyre, famous for its trade and riches, and situated in an island, made a braver defence, and reduced him to greater perplexities, than all the rest of the Persian empire; so difficult is it for the greatest monarchs, who subdue absolute monarchies with ease, to conquer a maritime power situated in an island. The Roman republic subdued all the absolute monarchies with which it was surrounded. Never was it brought into any real danger, but by the free state of Carthage. It was not conquered at last by any of the neighbouring kings, but by one of its own citizens. While it preserved its freedom, the fiercest and most numerous armies of barbarians, from the northern regions of Europe, could make no impression on its dominions : but, being reduced to a despotic monarchy, this huge empire fell a prey to the posterity of those barbarians. In modern times, the free states in Switzerland have preserved their country and their constitution, in spite of all the absolute monarchs of Europe. About 200 years ago, a few provinces of the Spanish monarchy, being driven to it by oppression, formed themselves into a common-wealth, and, during a long war, withstood the whole power of Spain. In a later period, they bravely defended themselves against Lewis XIV.

XIV. and baffled all his attempts in the midft of his glory. Abfolute monarchs have often fubdued one another. The Tartarian Tamerlane, the defpotic lords of the Saracens and of the Turks, have over-run great tracts of the earth, and have deftroyed feebler defpotic monarchies, corrupted with vice and luxury. But examples of free ftates falling before abfolute monarchies are very rare. Were the French remarkably lefs corrupted than the Britifh, Britain would have more to fear. But when it is acknowledged, that the manners of the French are as vain and as effeminate, as thofe of the Britifh, it is not the defpotifm of France, and the freedom of the Britifh government, that will give the French the advantage. In truth, if we may be allowed to form conjectures about the times or the feafons, and about thofe grand events, which the great Father of the world hath put only in his own power, it is not Britain, that ought to tremble for fear of France ; but France, that ought to dread the bravery and naval ftrength of the free Britons, if their juft indignation fhould be roufed to ftrike home and avenge the wrongs of their country. God forbid, that fo great, fo free, fo happy a nation, as Britain, fhould be fo impious and fo ungrateful towards God, or fo

un-

unjuft to themfelves and their pofterity, as
not to be of good courage, and to behave
themfelves valiantly for their people and the
cities of their God * !

* 1 Chronicles, XIX. 13.

POSTSCRIPT.

When the firft Edition of the Charac-
terifticks was publifhed, the writer did
not know, who was the author of the
three Effays, quoted page 17th of the firft
Edition, and in feveral other places of the
book.   And thefe Effays, having been
publifhed together, in one Pamphlet, in
the year 1755. In mentioning them, he ufed
the expreffion, " The author or the writer
of the three Effays."   But fince that time,
being affured by the beft authority, that the
author of the firft Effay, " On the publick
debt" was not the author of the fecond and
third Effays ; and that there are in the third
Effay, " On frugality" things, which are
intirely difagreeable to the fentiments of the
author

author of the firſt : the author of the Cha-
racteriſticks thinks it his duty to acquaint
his readers of this fact.   As for the ſecond
and third Eſſays, he does not know, whether
they were written by the ſame perſon or
not.

FINIS.